Wye Valley and Forest of Dean

Walks

Fully revised by
Dennis and Jan Kelsall

Text: Dennis and Jan Kelsall
Photography: Crimson Publishing, David Hancock and
                Dennis and Jan Kelsall
Editorial: Ark Creative UK Ltd
Design: Ark Creative UK Ltd

This product includes mapping data licensed from Ordnance Survey® with the permission of the Controller of Her Majesty's Stationery Office. © Crown Copyright 2011. All rights reserved. Licence number 150002047. Ordnance Survey, the OS symbol and Pathfinder are registered trademarks and Explorer, Landranger and Outdoor Leisure are trademarks of the Ordnance Survey, the national mapping agency of Great Britain.

ISBN: 978-1-85458-570-7

While every care has been taken to ensure the accuracy of the route directions, the publishers cannot accept responsibility for errors or omissions, or for changes in details given. The countryside is not static: stiles can be changed to gates, hedges and fences can be removed, field boundaries can alter, footpaths can be rerouted and changes in ownership can result in the closure or diversion of some concessionary paths. Also, paths that are easy and pleasant for walking in fine conditions may become slippery, muddy and difficult in wet weather, while stepping stones across rivers and streams may become impassable.

If you find an inaccuracy in either the text or maps, please write to Crimson Publishing at the address below.

First published 1991 by Jarrold Publishing. Revised and reprinted 1994, 1998, 2003, 2005, 2007, 2009, 2011

Printed in Singapore. 8/11

First published in Great Britain 2011 by Crimson Publishing, a division of:
Crimson Business Ltd,
Westminster House, Kew Road, Richmond, Surrey, TW9 2ND

www.totalwalking.co.uk

A catalogue record for this book is available from the British Library.

Front cover: The view from the top of Symonds Yat
Previous page: Chepstow Castle – formidable border stronghold

Contents

Walking Safety; Walkers and the Law; Countryside Access Charter; Useful Organisations; Ordnance Survey Maps

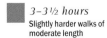

Up to 2½ hours	3–3½ hours	4 hours and over
Short walks on generally clear paths	Slightly harder walks of moderate length	Longer walks including some steep ascents/descents, occasionally on faint paths

The walk times are provided as a guide only and are calculated using an average walking speed of 2½mph (4km/h), adding one minute for each 10m (33ft) of ascent, and then rounding the result to the nearest half hour.

Walks are considered to be dog friendly unless specified.

Priory Wood, Clifford, Pen-y-Park, Merbach, Old Court, Brobury, Staunton on Wye, Lacy, Tillington

HAY-ON-WYE **19**, Cusop, Hardwicke, The Bage, Bredwardine **14**, Moccas Court, Mansell Gamage, Brinsop, Bishopstone, Burghill, Credenhill

Llanigon, Moccas, Monnington on Wye, Byford, Bridge Sollers, Kenchester, Swainshill, Stretton Sugwas, Upper Breinton

Dorstone, Preston on Wye, Blakemere, Canon Bridge, Ruckhall, King's Acre, Lower Breinton

Snodhill, Tyberton, Madley, Eaton Bishop, Clehonger, Belmon, Abbe

Hay Bluff **28**, Craswall, Michaelchurch Escley, Peterchurch, Shenmore, Vowchurch, Kingstone, Allensmore, A465

Capel-y-ffin, Upper Maes-coed, St Margarets, Newton, Bacton, Kerry's Gate, Cockyard, Didley, King's Thorn, Dewch

THE BLACK MOUNTAINS, Middle Maes-coed, Lower Maes-coed, Abbey Dore, Wormbridge, Kilpeck, Orcop Hill

Llanthony Priory, Llanthony **26**, Longtown Castle, Longtown, Ewyas Harold **16**, Pontrilas, Howton, Bagwyllydiart, Garway Hill, Orcop

Clodock, Crossway, Walterstone, Langua, Kentchurch, Kentchurch Court, Garway, St Weonards

Oldcastle, Cwmyoy, Pandy, Grosmont, Grosmont Castle, Hoaldalbert, White Rocks, Skenfrith Castle, Skenfrith **5**, Broa

Partrishow, Stanton, Llanvihangel Crucorney, Llangattock Lingoed, Cross Ash, Crossway, Newcastle, Llanrothal, Wels, Newt

Crickhowell, Crug Mawr, Forest Coal Pit, Bettws, Penyclawdd Court, Llanvihangel Court, Bont, Maypole, Llangattock Vibon-Avel

Llangenny, Llanbedr, Mynydd Pen-y-fal Sugar Loaf, Allt, Llantilio Pertholey, White Castle **1**, Llanvetherine, Llanvihangel Ystern-Llewern, Dingestow, MONMOUT TREFYN

Glangrwyney, Cwrt Y gollen, Mardy, ABERGAVENNY/Y FENNI, Llantilio Crossenny, Llanddewi Rhydderch, Llanvapley, Penrhos, Pen-yr-heol, Tregare, Wonastow, Caer Llan

Llanelly, Gilwern, Govilon, Llanfoist, Blorenge, Llanvaples, Wernrheolydd, Coed Morgan, Llanarth, Bryngwyn, A40, Raglan Castle, Pen-y-clawdd, Cwmcarvan

Clydach, NTYGLO, West Side, BLAENAVON, The Bryn, Llanvihangel Gobion, Llanover, Pencroesoped, Llanfair Kilgeddin, Raglan, Kingcoed, Llangovan

BLAINA, Forge Side, Varteg, Cwmavon, Nant-y-derry, Bettws Newydd, Twyn-y-Sheriff, Llanishen, Llansoy

ABERTILLERY, Cwmtillery, Mynydd Garnclochdy, Penperlleni, Kemeys Commander, Llancayo, Gwehelog, Llandenny, Gwernesney, Trelleck Grange

Aberbeeg, Snatchwood, Abersychan, Croes y pant, Little Mill, Usk Castle, A449

St Illtyd, Brynithel, Llanhilleth, Trevethin, Cwm Ffrwd-oer, Tranch, PONTYPOOL, Monkswood, USK, Slough, Llangwm, New Inn

Trinant, Swffryd, Griffithstown, Sebastopol, New Inn, Glascoed, Greenmeadow, Wolvesnewton, Dev

Oakdale, Crumlin, Penmaen, A4042, Llanllowell, Gaer-fawr, Kilgwrrwg Common, Newchurch, Chepsto

LANFRAITH, ABERCARN, Ynysddu, Castell-y-bwch, Croes-y-mwyalch, Llanhennock, Penhow, Llanvair Discoed, Shirenewton

Pontywaun, Cwmfelinfach, Wattsville, Crosskeys, Pontymister, RISCA, Malpas, CAERLEON, Christchurch, Langstone, Llandevaud, Wentwood

---

SCALE 1:250 000 or 1 INCH to 4 MILES *1CM to 2.5KM*

KILOMETRES: 0 2 4 6 8 10 15

MILES: 0 2 4 6 8 10

KEYMAP HEIGHTS SHOWN IN METRES

Keymap

Walk	Page	Start	Nat. Grid Reference	Distance	Time	Height Gain
Abbey Dore, Ewyas Harold & the Dulas Valley	47	Abbey Dore	SO 386303	6¼ miles (10.1km)	3 hrs	870ft (265m)
Bredwardine, Arthur's Stone and Merbach Hill	41	Bredwardine	SO 334445	6 miles (9.7km)	3 hrs	855ft (260m)
Chepstow and Lancaut	22	Chepstow	ST 535941	4½ miles (7.2km)	2½ hrs	835ft (255m)
Dymock and Kempley Green	76	Queen's Wood	SO 678284	9½ miles (15.3km)	4½ hrs	425ft (130m)
Fownhope, Brockhampton and Capler Camp	62	Fownhope	SO 578340	7½ miles (12.1km)	4 hrs	1,115ft (340m)
Goodrich Castle	59	Goodrich	SO 575195	8¼ miles (13.3km)	3½ hrs	310ft (95m)
Hay-on-Wye, Mouse Castle Wood and Cusop	56	Hardwicke	SO 263439	7¾ miles (12.5km)	3½ hrs	785ft (240m)
King's Caple, Sellack and Hoarwithy	30	King's Caple	SO 559288	5 miles (8km)	2½ hrs	375ft (115m)
Llanthony Priory and Hatterrall Hill	80	Llanthony Priory	SO 288278	8¾ miles (14.1km)	4½hrs	1,510ft (460m)
Monmouth and the Kymin	53	Monmouth	SO 504125	7 miles (11.3km)	3½ hrs	835ft (255m)
Mordiford and Haugh Wood	36	Mordiford	SO 567375	6 miles (9.7km)	3 hrs	590ft (180m)
Newent and Acorn Wood	28	Newent	SO 721259	5 miles (8km)	2½ hrs	360ft (110m)
New Fancy and Mallards Pike Lake	26	New Fancy picnic site	SO 627095	4¾ miles (7.6km)	2½ hrs	705ft (215m)
Newland	14	Newland	SO 553095	3 miles (4.8km)	1½ hrs	425ft (130m)
Newnham and Soudley Ponds	65	Newnham	SO 693120	8¼ miles (13.3km)	4 hrs	885ft (270m)
Penallt and Millstone Country	18	Redbrook	SO 536099	4¼ miles (6.8km)	2½ hrs	805ft (245m)
Ruardean and Aston- bridgehill Inclosure	38	Cannop Valley Speculation	SO 613136	6 miles (9.7km)	3 hrs	705ft (215m)
Skenfrith and Garway	20	Skenfrith	SO 456202	4½ miles (7.2km)	2½ hrs	540ft (165m)
Speech House, Cannop Ponds and Edge End	72	Speech House picnic site	SO 623124	8½ miles (13.7km)	4 hrs	1,015ft (310m)
St Briavels and Hewelsfield	69	St Briavels	SO 558046	8½ miles (13.7km)	4 hrs	970ft (295m)
Sugar Loaf	33	Sugar Loaf	SO 268167	5½ miles (8.9km)	3 hrs	1,475ft (450m)
Symonds Yat and Highmeadow Woods	84	Symonds Yat Rock	SO 562156	9¼ miles (14.9km)	4½ hrs	1,525ft (465m)
Tidenham Chase and Wintour's Leap	50	Tidenham Chase	ST 558992	6½miles (10.5km)	3½ hrs	755ft (230m)
Tintern Abbey and the Devil's Pulpit	44	Tintern	SO 528005	6 miles (9.7km)	3 hrs	985ft (300m)
The Upper Honddu Horseshoe	88	Gospel Pass	SO 236350	10½ miles (16.9km)	5½ hrs	1,920ft (585m)
Wench Ford, Danby Lodge & Blackpool Bridge	24	Wench Ford picnic site	SO 654079	4¾ miles (7.6km)	2½ hrs	690ft (210m)
White Castle	12	White Castle	SO 380168	2½ miles (4km)	1½ hrs	410ft (125m)
Wynd Cliff	16	Upper Wyndcliff	ST 524972	3¾ miles (6km)	2 hrs	755ft (230m)

Comments

Cistercian monks discovered the beauty of the Golden Valley, explored here in a walk through Ewyas Harold to the neighbouring and equally pretty Dulas valley.

King Arthur might never have existed, but the burial chamber bearing his name atop the high ground above Bredwardine is an impressive monument.

One of the first castles built after the Norman invasion, Chepstow begins this dramatic walk into the Wye gorge to the ruin of an ancient riverside chapel.

A profusion of wild daffodils makes this a favourite springtime ramble through a landscape much loved by the early 20th-century Dymock Poets.

An imposing Iron Age fort and splendid village church from the Arts and Crafts period are among the highlights of this enjoyable woodland and riverside walk.

Two of the forest's best-known features, Goodrich Castle and Symonds Yat come together on this walk through a spectacular section of the Wye Valley gorge.

Attractive Hay-on-Wye is the objective here, approached over rolling hills from Hardwicke past a Norman motte-and- bailey and a woodland nature reserve.

Many tiny villages scatter the Herefordshire countryside, the three linked here overlook a sharp bend of the Wye and each have a noteworthy church.

The picturesque setting of Llanthony Priory is just one of the endearing sights seen on this superb ramble that culminates in a fine ridge-walk above the valley.

When Nelson visited Monmouth, the people took him to their heart, erecting a monument to their great admirals on Kymin Hill, a superb viewpoint above the town.

Mordiford's bridge is the oldest in Herefordshire and is the start point for this circuit to nearby Haugh Wood, noted for its butterflies

This short walk from an attractive small town at the edge of the forest gives a fine panorama to the Malvern Hills.

Once one of the largest coalmines in the forest, New Fancy is the centre of a geopark, its spoil heap a lookout for bird-watchers searching for goshawks.

A relaxing valley and woodland walk starting from an attractive village with an imposing church that has justly been dubbed the 'Cathedral of the Forest'.

Once a bustling port beside the River Severn, Newnham is the start point of this foray into the eastern fringes of the Forest of Dean.

Sitting above the steep, wooded bank of the Wye, Penallt was once quarried for millstones but is now a quiet backwater of narrow paths and old lanes.

Traces of the forest's industrial past are not always easy to spot on this forest walk to Ruardean, a former coal mining and ore-smelting village.

Two defensible churches and an unusual medieval castle feature on this countryside ramble, which gives engaging views over the Monnow valley.

The ever-changing facets of the working forest are revealed on this walk from the 17th-century Speech House, during which you may see deer or wild boar.

Medieval churches, a castle and Offa's Dyke are all featured on this extended circuit from St Briavels, once the administrative centre of the Forest of Dean.

This simple ascent onto Sugar Loaf reveals stunning views and is followed by a pleasant saunter into the pretty, wooded valley of St Mary's Vale.

The view from Symonds Yat may be the most famous in the forest, but it is by no means the only striking spectacle as revealed in this glorious woodland ramble.

Woodland, heath and open countryside are combined with a well-preserved stretch of Offa's Dyke and memorable views across the Wye and Severn valleys.

'Discovered' by the Romantics, Tintern is included on this stretch through the Wye gorge that returns along a particularly striking section of Offa's Dyke.

This demanding day onto Hay Bluff and Twmpa at the head of the Vale of Ewyas includes a steep descent to Capel-y-ffin in the secluded heart of the valley.

From a delightful picnic spot beside Blackpool Brook, this meandering route passes one of Charles II's forest lodges and an ancient forest road.

A fine moated castle stands at the focus of this simple ramble, which reveals expansive views across the Welsh borderlands.

Follow in the footsteps of the Wye's first tourists, climbing the '365 steps' to the top of Wynd Cliff to share their favourite viewpoints across the gorge.

Introduction to the Wye Valley and Forest of Dean

Springing from a source high on the slopes of Plynlimon in the Cambrian Mountains, the River Wye flows for some 185 miles before finding eventual release in the Severn at Chepstow. Although Welsh by birth it is an English river too and after escaping from the rugged highlands, revels in the gentle beauty of the Herefordshire countryside before rushing to a climactic finish through a deep and twisting gorge, where its duality is acknowledged in defining the border between the two countries. Although the fifth longest river in Britain, the Wye is untouched by industry and passes through few towns of any appreciable size. Consequently, it is one of the cleanest major waterways in the country and supports a huge variety of plant and animal life, both within its unpolluted waters and along the valley through which it flows. It is a river of great and contrasting beauty and its precious qualities are recognised in the entire length being protected within a Site of Special Scientific Interest. Furthermore, the Wye's lower section has been designated as an Area of Outstanding Natural Beauty.

Undeniably delightful throughout its length, the river is at its most magnificent writhing in its final section through the gorge to Chepstow and it was to here that the first tourists came in 1783 clutching Gilpin's newly published Observations on the River Wye.

The whole area is grand walking country and explored here are the middle and lower reaches of the river, taking in some of the border country that lies to either side: the fringes of the Black Mountains from which emanate some of the Wye's prettiest tributary valleys; and the Forest of Dean, a unique and ancient woodland draping a high plateau above its confluence with the Severn. Borderlands are often rich in both their landscape and cultural history and these southern Marches are no exception. The countryside is everywhere compellingly attractive and in places, positively dramatic, a splendid backdrop to a diverse heritage that chronicles man's presence over the millennia.

Walking through history

The earliest evidence of human habitation in the area has been found in caves below Symonds Yat, perhaps the most spectacular stretch of the whole river, showing that bands of Palaeolithic hunter-gatherers moved along the valley as the climate improved after the last ice age, some 10,000 years ago. But it is not until a more settled lifestyle based on farming developed during the New Stone Age that man began to leave his mark on the landscape. The cromlech known as Arthur's Stone on the high ground dividing the Golden Valley from the Wye is the most impressive monument remaining from this period but there are many others such as the Long Stone in the Forest of Dean. Territorial identification and possession became increasingly important and by the time of the Iron Age many hilltops had been exploited as settlement, refuge and fort sites. Defined by prodigious earthworks encircling the summit, they were both imposing and functional and despite the passage of time, many like that at Capler still have the capacity to stir the imagination.

The Romans sought to conquer the whole country, but as had happened in the far north, they failed to subdue the native British tribes of Wales. Their civilising influence extended little farther west than the Wye, but they were happy to exploit the rich iron ore deposits of the Forest of Dean plateau. And while few traces of their settlements and villas remain, the practice of cultivating vines still continues and there are vineyards close to the walks onto Sugar Loaf Mountain and at Tintern.

The Anglo-Saxons fared little better in conquering the Welsh and, in establishing the western limit of his kingdom, the 8th-century Mercian King Offa defined a boundary between the two countries that set the pattern for the future. Running between the Severn and the Dee, it incorporates natural barriers and features, but lengthy sections take the form of a deep ditch protecting an earth embankment. The Dyke, more probably a political statement rather than a defensible border, was nonetheless a mighty undertaking and emphasises the power and organisational capability of this remarkable ruler. Two of the walks in the book follow impressive sections of the dyke above the wooded Wye gorge.

The 11th century saw the arrival of the Normans and here as elsewhere; they consolidated their position in formidable castles. Within a year of their first landing, the castle at Chepstow was founded to control an already important seaport. Others followed over the next two centuries, Monmouth, Goodrich, St Briavels and the 'trilateral' castles of White Castle, Skenfrith and Grosmont. Having strategic importance they were rebuilt in stone, but in other places such as Hay-on-Wye, Bredwardine and Ewyas Harold, the fortifications were never developed beyond the original motte-and-bailey. However, it was not until the latter part of the 13th century under Edward I - Edward Longshanks that Wales was finally brought under English rule and peace finally settled upon the borders.

The Normans were not only castle builders and their architectural skills are equally evident in their religious buildings. Christianity had long been established in Wales, several churches in the area bear dedication to the Welsh and Irish saints and one of the pilgrim routes to St David's passed through the Vale of Ewyas. The new nobility, partly as an investment for their spiritual future, endowed both money and land to the Church and here founded monastic houses at Monmouth, Tintern, and Llanthony and at Abbey Dore in the Golden Valley. What remains of Abbey Dore gives an insight into the splendour of the original building, and continues in use as the village church and as an occasional atmospheric venue for concert recitals. The Dissolution, however, reduced both Llanthony and Tintern to ruins, but each has a superb setting. Tintern was an inspiration to both Turner and Wordsworth, and helped promote the valley as one of the first British 'tourist' destinations during the 18th century.

Many village churches date from the medieval period and, usually being the oldest building, stand at the focus of the community and its history. All Saints at Newland is a massive edifice and has been dubbed the 'Cathedral of the Forest'. Although not nearly so old and very different is the tiny chapel at Capel-y-ffin, one of the smallest in the country. Another little church is at Cwmyoy on the climb to Hatterrall Hill from the stunningly beautiful Vale of Ewyas. Despite the ground on which it was built not having stopped moving during the 700 years of its existence, it miraculously remains standing and must be one of the most contorted buildings in existence. 'Modern' churches feature too in this collection in the splendid Arts and Crafts thatched building at Kempley Court, constructed at the beginning of the 19th century. By contrast on the same walk is the redundant St Mary's, which contains some of the finest early medieval frescoes in Britain.

With a gentle climate and rich soils, agriculture has always been important to the area, a rural lifestyle that has left a legacy of charming villages and small market towns. Cider production was a particularly important activity and even today large swathes of the countryside are devoted to orchards. Several of the walks pass a resurrected cider press, the stone quarried from the hills at Penallt being particularly suitable for the purpose.

The Forest of Dean

The Forest of Dean deserves special mention, for it was proclaimed a royal forest under William I and has remained so ever since. Continuing a precedent set by the Anglo-Saxon rulers, it was a hunting demesne reserved to the king and originally governed from the castle at St Briavels under a special code of law that protected both the forest and the game that roamed within. The forest became a valuable source of income to the Crown, with rights being licensed to the local nobility and those living within its bounds. A complex tariff of fees and fines gave peasants rights to gather firewood, graze animals or even cut a limited amount of timber while the aristocracy could gain a licence to hunt or exploit the timber and mineral resources.

Discovered before the arrival of the Romans, the extensive deposits of iron ore have been worked ever since. Later, stone was quarried to build castles and churches and after Edward I bestowed rights to anyone born within the forest, mining for coal became a major activity too. The forest trees not only provided charcoal to fuel the smelting process, but ancient oaks were felled to build war galleons for the Tudor navy. By the time the monarchy was re-instituted after the Civil War much of the forest had been denuded. Charles II ordered extensive replanting and built Speech House as the new centre for the forest's administration. Even so, the 19th-century Napoleonic Wars exposed the country's lack of shipbuilding timber and Nelson himself highlighted the need for more oaks to be planted in the forest. He could not have foreseen that by the time they came to maturity, naval architects would no longer be designing warships built of wood.

The First World War again demonstrated the country's dependency upon imported timber and in consequence the Forestry Commission was established. Some conifers had previously been introduced, but only now did large-scale softwood plantation begin to change the woodland character of the forest. More recently the trend has been reversed and broad-leaved trees constitute over half its area. Although it remains a commercial forest producing over 70,000 cubic metres of timber a year, equal importance is given to managing a mixed habitat that encourages a diversity of woodland wildlife.

Wandering through the woods today, it is hard to imagine how the place would have looked a century ago. During the 19th century, coal mining, iron production and quarrying were all major industries and the forest was criss-crossed with busy mineral tramways and railway lines that carried out their products. A geomap at the site of the New Fancy Mine shows how the different outcrops are distributed and lists 35 iron ore mines, 100 coalmines, nearly 50 major quarries and even a gold mine that once operated within the forest. Many, however, were small undertakings and walking almost anywhere in the forest you are likely to come upon disused quarry floors and faces, the hollows of old mines or rounded tips of spoil and furnace slag. Since their abandonment Nature has softened their lies and it is often difficult to recognise them for what they were. The course of an old railway is usually easier to spot in straight, level paths, cuttings and embankments and still-standing bridges and tunnel portals. Industrial decline set in during the early 20th century, and by the end of the Second World War, iron mining had finished. The last deep coal mine closed in 1965 and with no goods to carry, the railways gradually disappeared too. Although stone is still quarried and a handful of freeminers continue to exercise their ancient rights, the industrial heyday has long past, and it is now only in the area's museums that the extent of the activity is vividly revealed.

The River Wye

Through it all weaves the Wye, historically the highway of the region. The Romans built the first bridge across the river at Chepstow and there were numerous ferry crossings farther upstream. The river is tidal to Brockweir and was navigable as far as Monmouth and for centuries, barges carried cargoes up and down the river between small landings. The vessels might be sailed or more usually hauled upstream, but coming back could take advantage of the current. Even so, this was hard and dangerous work, particularly when the river was in spate and drowning was not an uncommon fate for the barge hands. During the 17th century, the river was improved to enable boats to reach Hereford and eventually Hay-on-Wye, thus opening the hinterland to trade. With the 19th century came the railway, repeatedly crossing the river on bridges and shortcutting the tight loops through tunnels as it followed the Wye through the valley.

The railways have now gone and, apart from the canoes drifting lazily downstream in summer, so too have the boats. Even the road is absent from many stretches of the river and the only way to appreciate the valley and its surroundings is on foot. The area is blessed with a fine network of paths, tracks and quiet lanes that opens up the Wye's beautiful countryside, explored in this collection of walks, which range between the long ridges at the edge of the Black Mountains and the lush woodlands of Dean.

This book includes a list of waypoints alongside the description of the walk, so that you can enjoy the full benefits of gps should you wish to. For more information on using your gps, read the *Pathfinder® Guide GPS for Walkers,* by gps teacher and navigation trainer, Clive Thomas (ISBN 978-0-7117-4445-5). For essential information on map reading and basic navigation, read the *Pathfinder® Guide Map Reading Skills* by outdoor writer, Terry Marsh (ISBN 978-0-7117-4978-8). Both titles are available in bookshops or can be ordered online at www.totalwalking.co.uk

White Castle

			GPS waypoints
Start	White Castle		⬛ SO 380 168
Distance	2½ miles (4km)		Ⓐ SO 376 166
Height gain	410 feet (125m)		Ⓑ SO 371 169
Approximate time	1½ hours		Ⓒ SO 364 172
Parking	Near entrance to White Castle		Ⓓ SO 372 177
Route terrain	Field paths and quiet lane		
Ordnance Survey maps	Landranger 161 (The Black Mountains), Explorer OL13 (Brecon Beacons National Park – Eastern area)		

White Castle occupies a hilltop overlooking the valley of the River Trothy, a tributary of the Wye. The short walk drops across the fields to the nearby village of Llanvetherine, returning along a section of the Three Castles Walk past the site of an old mill.

Of the three 'Trilateral' castles, Grosmont, Skenfrith and White Castle, this is the most striking, although it has lost the white rendering that gave it its name. They were built to consolidate Norman rule in the area and were held under a single lord as the Honour of Grosmont. Like the others, White Castle was probably founded in the 11th century as a moated earthwork with a stone keep being added soon after. It was remodelled in the 12th and 13th centuries to meet the threat posed by Llewelyn ap Gruffudd. But after Edward I subdued Wales, the castle saw only

White Castle

brief action in 1404 during the unsuccessful rising of Owain Glyndŵr against the English crown. The castle remained in use as a residence and during the middle of the 15th century Henry VI undertook repairs to its fabric. However, it was abandoned some time after to become a ruin and was eventually given to the State in 1922.

It is easily the most visually impressive of the three, but you must go inside the walls to appreciate its full extent. Overlooking a deep and now-dry ditch, the ruin of an impressive gatehouse guards the entrance to the outer ward, a general area for stabling, storage and training. Behind it lies the heart of the castle, encircled by a further moat and formidable walls strung between stout towers. Within lay the great hall, kitchens and living quarters for the nobles.

🖉 A track in front of the ticket office waymarked as Offa's Dyke Path skirts the castle walls to pass a cottage. Through a small gate at the end, enter the corner of a field and follow the

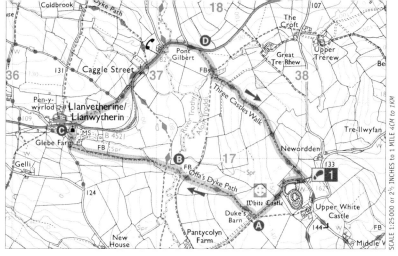

boundary to the right. Approaching the far end, turn right through a gate **A** and walk behind a cottage. A little farther along, slip through a gate and continue on the other side of the hedge. Passing through the hedge once more at another gate lower down, bear left, striking a shallow angle from the left hedge. Aiming towards the left end of Ysgyryd Fawr, the distinct hill in the middle distance, head downfield to find a gate about halfway along the bottom fence. Cross a narrow pasture to a footbridge spanning the River Trothy **B**.

A trod beyond guides you to an indented corner. There abandon the Offa's Dyke Path and bear slightly left across the field to another bridge in the middle of the far hedge. Follow the boundary around to the right, the church at Llanvetherine soon coming into view. Carry on to the far side of a second field, there crossing a gravel drive to continue ahead behind a converted barn. Leave over a stile beside a gate onto an old, hedged way and turn right. At the end, go over a bridge and stone stile into the churchyard of St James the Elder, walking around the eastern side of the church out to a lane **C**.

Cross to a stile directly opposite and strike a right diagonal to the top corner of the field. Pass through a gap into the field above and immediately turn right over a stile beside a gate. Bearing slightly left, head to a stile in the far hedge and keep going along a margin of trees. Leave over a stile and follow a tarmac track down past the houses of Caggle Street to a lane at the bottom.

Turn left and follow the lane for a little over ¼ mile, crossing a bridge and then shortly passing a junction. Some 100 yds farther on, abandon it over a stile on the right **D**. Waymarked the Three Castles Walk, a trod falls beside a ditch to trees at the bottom of the field, where a footbridge spans a stream. Just to the left is the site of the Great Trerhew Farm Mill, thought to have originally been built in the 13th century to supply the castle. Although the castle had been abandoned by the early 1500s, the mill continued to operate until the end of the 19th century, but no doubt it would have been rebuilt several times by then.

On the eastern bank, climb right to a stile and head steadily uphill from field to field beside the hedge. An old sunken way shaded by trees develops in the top field, which leads to a stile at the corner of a wood. The ongoing path running beside it returns you to the parking area by the castle.   ●

Newland

		GPS waypoints	
Start	Newland		SO 553 095
Distance	3 miles (4.8km)	**Ⓐ**	SO 550 093
Height gain	425 feet (130m)	**Ⓑ**	SO 547 091
Approximate time	1½ hours	**Ⓒ**	SO 549 079
Parking	Limited roadside parking in village		
Route terrain	Woodland paths and farm tracks		
Ordnance Survey maps	Landranger 162 (Gloucester & Forest of Dean), Explorer OL14 (Wye Valley & Forest of Dean)		

Beginning from one of the Forest of Dean's prettiest villages, this short walk explores a secluded side valley off the River Wye. Twisting in a tight loop overlooked by thick woods bristling the high bluffs, its lower pastures exude an almost alpine character. After mounting the ridge separating the arms of the horseshoe-shaped vale, the route follows the stream, known simply as Valley Brook, before climbing back into the village.

One of the oldest villages in the forest, Newland drapes across a steep hillside,

Newland church, the 'Cathedral of the Forest'

its neat cottages lining narrow lanes that radiate from the church and pub. Dubbed the 'Cathedral of the Forest' and set within a spacious graveyard bounded by an attractive row of 17th-century almshouses built to accommodate eight men and eight women of Newland together with a lecturer, is All Saints Church. Dean was a royal forest and this imposing church emphasises the importance of those involved in its building, which included Edward I who added a small chapel in 1305.

The many funerary monuments reflect forest society: local aristocracy, foresters, miners and farmers. Among them is one to Jenkin Wyrall, Forester of Fee, who died in 1457 and is presented in his woodsman's tunic, carrying the tools of his trade; horn, sword and knife. Another treasure is an engraved brass depicting a knight's helmet crested with a hod-carrying miner holding a pick and grasping a candle between his teeth. It signifies the importance of mining to the community and has a parallel in Derbyshire, the stone carving of a lead miner, originally in St James' at Bonsall but now in Wirksworth's church.

 From **The Ostrich**, walk through the churchyard, exiting at its south-western corner. Head steeply down the lane facing you, appropriately named Savage Hill. Go right at the bottom and then bear right again at a fork **Ⓐ** past a paddock and small stable. Keep ahead on a narrow stone track, climbing steadily between high hedgebanks.

Reaching a junction at the crest **Ⓑ**, go left to a barrier and then immediately veer right between posts onto a path falling through Astridge Wood. Ignore a crossing partway down, shortly emerging at the bottom into a sloping meadow. Maintain your slanting descent to its distant corner, leaving through a gate to join a track cradled in the valley.

To the left it wanders undemandingly past a couple of ponds that trap the flow of the diminutive river. Higher up, cross the brook and then at a fork keep left. Where the main gravel way subsequently turns up towards a house, keep ahead through a gate on a grass track.

The track curves within the sweep of the valley, eventually passing below the mullion-windowed manor of Lodges Farm. Carry on, joining the track from the farm **Ⓒ** and re-crossing the stream above another pond, now drained. The rough lane climbs gently past alternating woodland and pasture for almost a mile before meeting your outward route at Greenbank Farm **Ⓐ**. Re-climb Savage Hill, and perhaps this time, detour past the almshouses to return to the pub. ●

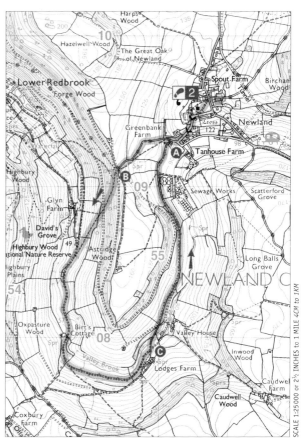

Wynd Cliff

		GPS waypoints	
Start	Upper Wyndcliff	✏ ST 524 972	
Distance	3¾ miles (6km)	Ⓐ ST 526 972	
Height gain	755 feet (230m)	Ⓑ ST 527 974	
Approximate time	2 hours	Ⓒ ST 529 992	
Parking	Car park at start	Ⓓ ST 523 985	
Route terrain	Woodland paths and field tracks	Ⓔ ST 525 980	
Dog friendly	Metal staircase towards top of '365 Steps'		
Ordnance Survey maps	Landranger 162 (Gloucester & Forest of Dean), Explorer OL14 (Wye Valley & Forest of Dean)		

The deep gorge of the Wye between Monmouth and Chepstow is undeniably dramatic and long-distance paths run on each side of the river as if to emphasise the point. To the east is the Offa's Dyke Path while on this bank is the Wye Valley Walk, loosely accompanying the river almost to its source on Plynlimon. The section followed here is particularly beautiful, seeking out viewpoints 'discovered' by the 18th-century Romantics.

The disruption of the Napoleonic Wars forced the genteel classes to look elsewhere for their grand tours and the Wye Valley was one of the first places to feature on the emergent British tourist trail. Egerton, Gilpin, Wordsworth, Turner and others excited imaginations with their writings and art, drawing people to experience the picturesque scenes at first-hand.

✏ There is a viewpoint at the start of the walk, reached by a short path to the right of the car park entrance. *You then have a choice of routes, both leaving from the back of the parking area.* To the left of the noticeboard, a climbing path winds through a hairpin to follow the upper edge of the woods direct to 'Eagles Nest'. It avoids the rough cliff path via the '365 Steps', which includes a section of metal staircase that dogs may find difficult.

The path to the right winds a steady descent through the wood to a disused quarry by the road. Cross to the Lower Wyndcliff car park Ⓐ, from the back of which is a superb view down the River Wye sweeping below the wooded Piercefield Cliffs.

Go back to the quarry and now take the path to the right, signed to the 365 Steps. The intermittently stepped path squirms between moss-draped boulders and trees steadily progressing towards the top of the cliffs, though whether there are actually 365 of them depends upon what you count. An opening partway up gives a taster of what to expect from the top, the soaring pylons of the Severn Road Bridge spanning both the Severn and the mouth of the Wye being a distinctive landmark.

Higher up, a metal staircase heralds the final section of the climb, which shortly meets the cliff-top path Ⓑ. Go right, soon reaching another junction, where the Eagles Nest viewpoint is just to the right. Anticipation is rewarded in a panorama that outdoes all the others. Against a backdrop of the Severn and the distant Cotswold Hills, the River Wye sweeps in a great 'S' bend around Lancaut and beneath the cliffs and quarries below Wintour's Leap.

Continue along the main path near the top edge of the woodland, unobtrusively relinquishing some of the height recently gained. Reaching a corner, keep left, ignoring the path dropping right. But then a little later on, where the path again forks at another corner, take the right branch, moving deeper into the woods. Farther on, disregard a crossing path from the fields and keep going between the trees above Black Cliff. Eventually, at the end of the long ridge, the path twists abruptly to a rocky, root-tangled descent. Soon veering right, the gradient eases, but watch for the path swinging left down to a track at the edge of the wood.

To the left, go through a gate into a pasture and head out half-left across the slope to a gate into more woodland at the far side **C**. A path leads away left, ending over a footbridge onto a crossing track. Now leaving the Wye Valley Walk, follow the old green lane left, which initially rises beside the course of a stream. Farther on it

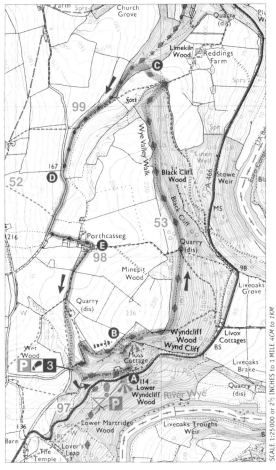

SCALE 1:25000 or 2½ INCHES to 1 MILE 4CM to 1KM

0	200	400	600	800 METRES	1

KILOMETRES
MILES

0	200	400	600 YARDS	½

progressively narrows before ultimately tipping you onto a quiet lane **D**.

Follow it left, gently uphill for ¼ mile to a junction, there going left again to Porthcasseg Farm. Reaching the farm, dogleg to remain with the main track ahead behind a converted barn, at the end of which **E**, swing right past an open barn. Walk forward through a gate and continue along a track across the fields. Rising over a crest, there is another view to the Severn Bridge, beyond which the track falls steadily to a gate and stile onto a lane. The car park is then just to the left. ●

Penallt and Millstone Country

Start	Redbrook		GPS waypoints
Distance	4¼ miles (6.8km)		🥾 SO 536 099
Height gain	805 feet (245m)		Ⓐ SO 526 106
			Ⓑ SO 520 096
Approximate time	2½ hours		Ⓒ SO 522 089
Parking	Car park at start		Ⓓ SO 534 090
Route terrain	Field paths and quiet lanes		
Ordnance Survey maps	Landranger 162 (Gloucester & Forest of Dean), Explorer OL14 (Wye Valley & Forest of Dean)		

Overlooking Redbrook from the west is the Penallt plateau, an area of quiet back lanes divorced from the busyness of modern life. This circuit climbs from the river to its ancient church, returning via Pen-twyn along a deepening side valley and then accompanying a stretch of the former Wye Valley Railway back to the start.

The Wye Valley Railway opened in 1876 between Chepstow and Monmouth, but was fated from the start for it offered no convenient links to the main valley industries, wire-drawing at Tintern, paper mills at Whitebrook and tinplate manufacture at Redbrook.

🖊 From the larger northern car park by the Wye at Redbrook, follow the river downstream beside a playing field. A short way along double back down to the river, crossing on a footbridge carried on the pillars of a disused railway bridge. Dropping to a lane at the far side, turn right past the **Boat Inn**. Just beyond, as the lane starts to climb, bear right through a gate on a path signed to Monmouth. Carry on beside the river from pasture to pasture, eventually entering Washing's Wood.

Partway through, look for a footpath slanting up to the left, rising steeply through the trees to emerge at the end of a track. Turn right to find a delightful old pathway, which continues the climb, eventually meeting a lane by Hillside Farm Ⓐ. Carry on, gaining height to a junction, from which Penallt Old Church lies to the right.

Strangely, the dedication has long been forgotten but tradition has it that it was made to St James. The oldest part standing is the tower erected in the 13th century and of interest inside is a squint passage that allows the congregation sitting in the south aisle to see the altar.

Return to the lane and walk uphill. The gradient soon levels and the way breaks from the trees, opening a superb view across the valley as it skirts around the woodland of Church Hill Common. Beside the lane, where a footpath leaves above Llananant Farm is the Cross Dermond Coffin Stone, upon which the coffin was laid while the bearers took rest and refreshment on their way to the burial.

Shortly after, the lane dips past a fine old stone barn and a junction. As the hill then steepens, look for a footpath signed off over a stile on the left. A path ascends easily through the trees. Through a gap near the corner of an old stone wall, the trees give way to bracken. By a waymark at the far side, the path veers right, gaining height to a stile onto another lane **B**.

Go left but after some 50 yds, leave along a rising track on the right signed to Pen y garn and Pen-twyn. In about 200 yds, turn over a stile on the left and follow the field boundary away. At the far side of the second field, the way continues as a hedged path. It ends across bracken beside a converted chapel, at a junction of lanes on the edge of Pen-twyn.

Walk forward and bear left along a narrow lane that leads to a small green in front of **The Inn at Penallt**. Bear right in front of the pub to leave along a grass track beside Pen-twyn cottage.

The old lane curves downwards to end at a tarmac lane **C**. Continue downhill for nearly ¾ mile and then look for wooden gates on the right, through which the River Wye is signed along a gravel drive.

In the garden below, an old apple press has been erected as a centre piece. It is a reminder that the area was once dependent on its many orchards from which cider was produced and also that millstones were cut from Penallt rock.

Where the drive bends, keep ahead, but after passing a wooden shed, fork left along a stepped path descending a steep wooded bank. At the bottom, continue down another drive to a track, the old rail bed. Over a stile opposite, a short path leads to the riverbank **D**. Turn left upstream back to the railway viaduct. Cross and return to the car park.

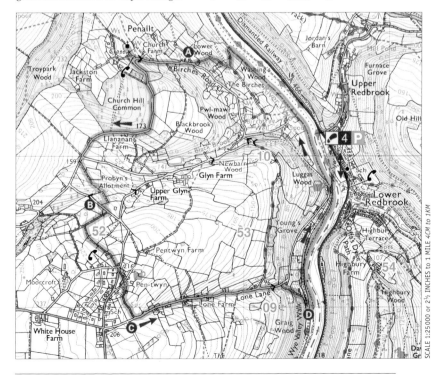

Skenfrith and Garway

		GPS waypoints
Start	Skenfrith	☑ SO 456 202
Distance	4½ miles (7.2km)	Ⓐ SO 459 203
Height gain	540 feet (165m)	Ⓑ SO 453 224
Approximate time	2½ hours	Ⓒ SO 465 226
Parking	Parking area in front of Skenfrith Castle	Ⓓ SO 462 217
Route terrain	Field paths and quiet lanes	
Ordnance Survey maps	Landranger 161 (The Black Mountains), Explorer 189 (Hereford & Ross-on-Wye)	

Beginning from Skenfrith Castle, the walk follows a quiet back lane rising above the River Monnow to the tiny hilltop village of Garway before returning across the fields. As well as the impressive ruins of the medieval fortification, the ancient churches of both settlements are also worthy of investigation.

Skenfrith, along with nearby Grosmont and White Castle have for most of their history been under the control of a single Lord. It has been suggested that the first earthworks at the three sites date from the 11th century as William Fitz Osbern brought the area under Norman control. However, the present fortifications are largely the work of Hubert de Burgh, regent of England after the death of King John until Henry III's majority in 1227. Skenfrith castle is somewhat unusual in having a circular keep, influenced by the architecture of the French castles Hubert de Burgh had seen while fighting in France.

Hubert also built the adjacent church, which is dedicated to the Irish St Bridget, and suggests that there may have been a church here before the Normans arrived. Her image appears on the lectern, carved by George Jack. Although born in America, he was of Scottish descent and returned to Britain to work as an architect and a furniture

designer for the William Morris company. Also inside the church is an assortment of fine pews, including two carved box pews from the 16th century. Displayed in a glass case is a beautifully embroidered 15th-century cope. Notice too the carved table tomb of John Morgan, Steward of the Duchy of Lancaster, a member of parliament and last governor of the 'Three Castles' until his death in 1557. He is depicted lying beside his wife, Anne and around the sides are eight kneeling weepers, presumably their children.

Walk back to the main road and turn left past **The Bell** to cross the River Monnow. At the next junction Ⓐ go left along a narrow lane that curves to run beside the river below a steep wooded bank. The lane shortly diverges from the river, climbing the hill towards Garway, whose scattered cottages later come into intermittent view. Ignore a turning off partway up, instead abandoning the lane just before the top along a track signed to Garway Church **B**.

Around 1180, Henry II granted Garway to the Knights Templar, whose church on the site of an earlier Saxon foundation took the form of a circular nave and square chancel. The heavy-set detached tower followed soon after and has the air of a fortress. Indeed, it was used as a refuge in case of attack by the Welsh in what were troubled times and then, somewhat later, served as a prison. After the order was disbanded the church was transferred to the Knights Hospitaller, who rebuilt the church in its present form, the connection of the tower to the body of the church only being made in the 17th century.

Walk past the church and a small garden behind, overlooked by an ancient well. Until around 1950, the spring, which supplied it, was one of the main water sources for the village and is probably the reason why the church was built here in the first place.

Through a gate cross what is now a rough meadow, glancing over to the right to see the medieval dovecote at the back of Church Farm. Continue past a derelict tennis court and over a stile into a field. Head straight across, bypassing left of a clump of trees and climbing to a stile in the top hedge. Over that, turn left and follow the edge of a couple of fields up to a lane. Go right through the linear village.

Beyond the **Garway Moon** at a

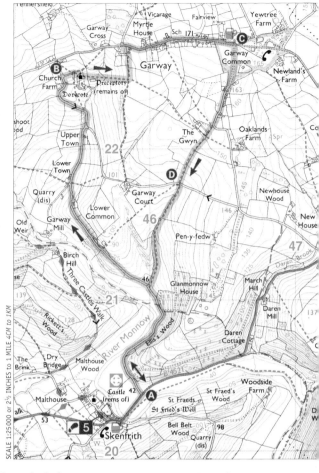

junction on the corner of the common **C**, go right towards Skenfrith and Abergavenny. Where the lane later swings abruptly left, bear right on a drive, taking the left fork as it then splits. Walk past a house, keeping left of its garage and a barn beyond. Continue down at the perimeter of a field, exiting through a gate at the end onto a lane **D**.

Cross to a stile opposite and carry on downhill. Keep going in a second field, emerging at the bottom onto a lane. Turn left to retrace your outward steps to Skenfrith. ●

Chepstow and Lancaut

Chepstow and Lancaut

		GPS waypoints
Start	Chepstow	☑ ST 535 941
Distance	4½ miles (7.2km)	Ⓐ ST 536 948
Height gain	835 feet (255m)	Ⓑ ST 539 955
Approximate time	2½ hours	Ⓒ ST 534 966
Parking	Car park by castle (Pay & Display)	Ⓓ ST 542 964
Route terrain	Field paths and quiet lanes, a short scramble across boulders	Ⓔ ST 542 956
Dog friendly	Some dogs may find the short boulder section difficult	
Ordnance Survey maps	Landrangers 162 (Gloucester & Forest of Dean) and 172 (Bristol & Bath), Explorer OL14 (Wye Valley & Forest of Dean)	

Just upstream of Chepstow, the River Wye flows through a deep-sided narrow gorge. This walk from the foot of the town's castle drops along it through a woodland nature reserve to the river, returning past the ruin of a medieval church and a spectacular viewpoint.

Chepstow controlled the lowest crossing point of the River Wye before it debouches into the River Severn. The earliest bridge may have been built by the Romans and it subsequently developed as a port and trading centre. The Normans recognised its strategic position on the border between England and Wales and within a year of his invasion, William commissioned a castle, the earliest stone fortress to survive in the country. It stood firm throughout the times of trouble between the Welsh and English and only fell in 1648 to the Parliamentarians during the Civil War.

🖉 From the car park, follow Bridge Street left down to the Wye Bridge. Cross the river, but as the road then swings left, keep ahead up a walled track. Halfway up, Offa's Dyke Path joins from the right climbing to a road at the top. Cross to the path opposite

and continue up Moplas Road. Curving around a bend, leave through a kissing-gate on the left Ⓐ.

A trod guides you up the field, passing near the top the ruin of a round tower in a garden to the right. It is apparently the remains of a windmill that was 'renovated' as a folly in the 19th century. Ahead, the narrowing tip of the field ushers you to a kissing-gate. Walk away at the edge of grazing to another kissing-gate in the corner. A walled path leads to a drive. Go right but after 30 yds, leave through yet another kissing-gate on the left and follow a trod across more pasture to a final gate at the far side Ⓑ.

To the left, a contained path runs underneath a small bridge into the Lancaut Nature Reserve. After descending steeply across the cliff through close-packed trees, the way briefly levels at the foot of an abandoned quarry. The stone was loaded into boats, taken down river and used, amongst other things in the building of Bristol's Avonmouth Docks.

Occasionally identified with red waymarks, the path continues downwards, later scrambling across a chaos of boulders, blasted from the Woodcroft Quarry above. *Take care over the rocks, the route indicated by yellow paint.* Back in thick woodland, ignore any paths climbing to the right. The main path shortly closes with the river and follows it around a sweeping bend.

Reaching the far end of the woods, the path passes below the ruin of St James Church and is then waymarked up beside the enclosure of its old graveyard. Although now isolated beside the river, nearby earthworks indicate that during the medieval period it was part of a small settlement. On the evidence of a lead font, now in the cathedral at Gloucester, it is thought that the church dates from the early decades of the 12th century.

From the top corner of the graveyard, take the path to the left, which runs a short distance through trees to come out over a stile at the bottom of a sloping field. Climb diagonally away to the top corner above Lancaut Farm.

Emerging there through a gate onto the end of a quiet lane **C**, follow it right for ¾ mile to reach the main road **D**. Head down to the right for some 250 yds passing a short track that leads to the dramatic viewpoint of Wintour's Leap.

A few yards beyond the track and immediately before the first cottage, fork off right onto Offa's Dyke Path. Pass behind the cottages above the precipitous cliff, although those with a tendency to vertigo will be thankful that the view is concealed behind a fringe of bushy trees. A little farther on however, the trees finish to reveal the massive

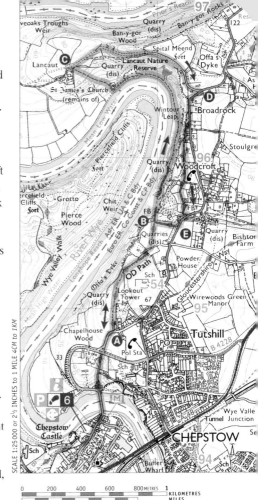

SCALE 1:25000 or 2½ INCHES to 1 MILE 4CM to 1KM

```
0      200    400    600   800 METRES   1
                                        KILOMETRES
                                        MILES
0      200    400   600 YARDS   ½
```

extent of the former quarry workings.

Meeting a track at the entrance to the quarry, cross and follow the descending path ahead in front of a bungalow. Lower down keep going through consecutive kissing-gates, ultimately passing beneath an arch bearing the curious inscription 'Mediaeval Times Donkey Lane' back onto the main road **E**.

Go right, watching for Offa's Dyke Path leaving again on the right after 100 yds. A contained path leads to the point at which you first entered the Lancaut Nature Reserve **B**. Pass through the kissing-gate and reverse your outward route in order to return to Chepstow.

Wench Ford, Danby Lodge and Blackpool Bridge

Start	Wench Ford picnic site	
Distance	4¾ miles (7.6km)	
Height gain	690 feet (210m)	
Approximate time	2½ hours	
Parking	Car park at start	
Route terrain	Woodland paths and tracks	
Ordnance Survey maps	Landranger 162 (Gloucester & Forest of Dean), Explorer OL14 (Wye Valley & Forest of Dean)	

GPS waypoints

- ✍ SO 654 079
- Ⓐ SO 651 079
- Ⓑ SO 646 082
- Ⓒ SO 645 088
- Ⓓ SO 651 089
- Ⓔ SO 657 098
- Ⓕ SO 653 088

Of the many picnic sites scattered throughout the forest, those beside water are justifiably the most popular. This circuit begins beside Blackpool Brook and climbs through the trees to Danby Lodge. There is a view from the ridge as the walk continues over wooded hills before returning past an ancient bridge and a preserved stretch of one of the forest's earliest paved roads.

✍ Take the path opposite the toilets to Blackpool Brook, following it downstream and turning out over a bridge to the road. Cross diagonally to a narrow path and immediately bear right at a fork, climbing gently into the trees. Meeting a broad foresters' road at the top of the rise Ⓐ, go right, winding with it for the best part of ½ mile. At a brief widening of the track, look for an unmarked path on the left, crossing a belt of bracken to the trees. Rising steadily, keep ahead, shortly intercepting a crossing path. Go left to reach a broad forest road.

Opposite to the left a path resumes the climb. Again go left when you meet another path Ⓑ, soon passing through a gate to follow a wall up to the entrance of Danby Lodge. Cross the drive and continue beside the perimeter wall to a crossing of tracks at the next

corner. Keep right with the wall.

Danby Lodge, was built at the same time as Speech House in the 1670s, as part of Charles II's revitalisation of the forest. Each housed a verderer responsible for an area of the forest called a 'walk'. The area surrounding Danby is pocked with the depressions of old coal mines and was the site of one of the last independent mines in the forest, which was working until just a few years ago.

Long before large-scale mining began during the 19th century, there was a tradition of 'free mining' in the forest. The right was bestowed by Edward I after forest miners helped him win the day in Northumberland by tunnelling beneath the walls of the castle at Berwick-upon-Tweed. Any man born within the Hundred of St Briavels, aged over 21 and who has worked in a mine for a year and a day can claim the right. Free mines worked alongside commercial enterprise throughout the 19th and 20th centuries, but the future of the practice is in doubt.

Carry on beyond the end of the wall to a junction and go left, the path gently descending along a broad ridge. At the far end, the path curves down left, dropping to a foresters' road.

Opposite is a minor path, its beginnings concealed in the bracken, but which quickly becomes more defined as it falls through the trees. Meeting a more prominent trail at the bottom, follow it left above the road. After 200 yds, look for a narrow path dropping towards the road. At the bottom go left and right, carefully clambering down a steep bank onto the carriageway **C**.

Go right for about 30 yds before climbing over a fence stile to a stone bridge spanning Blackpool Brook. Across, turn right, initially beside the stream, but soon moving away to gain height. Reaching a forest trail, turn right and follow it for ¼ mile.

Watch for a path forking left **D**, which rises gently beside a fence. Carry on as another shortly joins from below, eventually climbing out at the top over a stile onto another forest trail. Turn right, passing beside a barrier to emerge at a junction of lanes.

Cross to the one opposite, signed to Bradley Hill, turning off after 50 yds along a track on the right **E**. Where it later tops out at the crest of a rise, leave along a grass

path to the right. Later meeting a forest road, keep ahead, doing the same again when you encounter a crossing path. Very soon after that, the path swings right losing height more steeply to a track. Go right following it down to the road **F**.

Turn left to Blackpool Bridge, which has been suggested to be of Roman origin. Walking on, pass beneath a graceful bridge, built to carry the Forest of Dean Central Railway, which opened in 1868 to carry coal to the Severn from the collieries in the heart of the forest. However, competition from the Severn and Wye Railway thwarted its ambitions and the line finally closed in 1949. Just beyond, turn off left to follow the old trackbed back to Wench Ford. ●

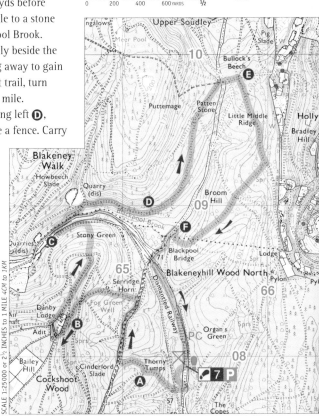

New Fancy and Mallards Pike Lake

		GPS waypoints
Start	New Fancy picnic site	
Distance	4¾ miles (7.6km)	📝 SO 627 095
Height gain	705 feet (215m)	Ⓐ SO 630 096
		Ⓑ SO 636 106
Approximate time	2½ hours	Ⓒ SO 645 102
Parking	Car park at start	Ⓓ SO 641 089
		Ⓔ SO 640 095
Route terrain	Woodland paths and tracks	Ⓕ SO 635 084
Ordnance Survey maps	Landranger 162 (Gloucester & Forest of Dean), Explorer OL14 (Wye Valley & Forest of Dean)	Ⓖ SO 628 091

The area around New Fancy and Mallards Pike Lake lay at the heart of industrial mining and quarrying in the forest. New Fancy was one of the largest mines, the remains of its spoil heap, now softened by vegetation, provide a panoramic view across the wooded valleys for bird-watchers on the lookout for goshawks.

📝 Leave the northern tip of the car park along the waymarked cycle trail, which drops to the line of an old tramway that served the pit. Go right, shortly reaching a crossing track and there turn left towards Dilke Bridge Ⓐ. Reaching an extended junction, keep ahead at a fork and then over a crossroads, the trackbed of the mineral loop of the Severn and Wye Railway. Some ¼ mile farther on there is another crossing path, optimistically levelled to carry the fated Forest of Dean Central Railway.

The Forest of Dean Central Railway Company had ambitions to serve the quarries and pits in the central part of the forest, linking them to a new wharf to be built on the Severn at Brims Pill. By 1869 the line was open as far as New Fancy from the Newport–Gloucester main line near Awre. But construction went no further, for in 1872, the Severn and Wye Railway opened a loop through the forest between Drybrook Road near Cinderford and Tufts Junction south of Whitecroft, from which the line continued to docks on the River Severn below Lydney. The Severn and Wye took the New Fancy contract, leaving the Central Railway with only Howbeach to serve.

Continue ahead, now on a lesser path that leads across a stream. Carry on steadily upwards through the trees, eventually reaching a junction Ⓑ. Turn right, heading downhill. Go over a forest trail to follow a narrower path that winds down to cross a stream before climbing away again to intersect another trail. Take the clear path opposite progressing between conifers and eventually meeting another trail. Cross diagonally left, the ongoing path still plodding straight up the hill to come out at the top onto a foresters' road opposite Staple-edge Bungalows Ⓒ.

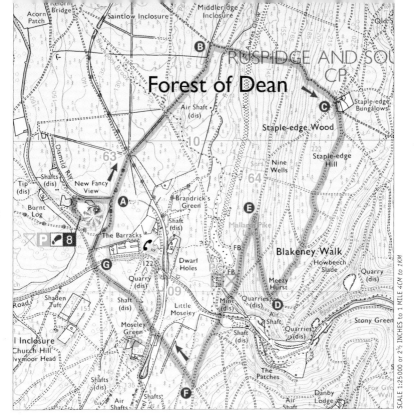

Turn right, but on a bend 50 yds along, go over a stile on the right from which a grassy path descends into the trees. When you reach a crossing track keep ahead, later doing the same again at a second crossing. The path then begins to descend more steeply and meets a forest road at the bottom **D**.

Go right and walk for a little over ¼ mile to another junction **E**, there doubling back sharp left downhill. The gravel road drops above the foot of Mallards Pike Lake, which is glimpsed through the trees. Keep ahead past a junction and then across a bridge over a deep cutting dug for the Forest of Dean Central Railway. Emerging onto a tarmac drive, follow it over a cattle-grid to meet a lane at the entrance to the Mallards Pike car park.

Take the barriered track opposite and climb to a crosspath at the crest of a rise overseen by an electricity post **F**. Turn sharp right, falling across a recently

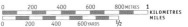

cleared area of forest to come out onto a lane near **The Rising Sun**. Go right past its drive but then immediately turn left along a barriered forest track. Keep ahead at a crossing, just to the right of which is a small fenced enclosure, one of the many coal pits scattered through the forest. Carry on over the rise of the hill, where, for the time being at least, felling has opened an expansive view.

Emerging at a road junction **G**, take the lane opposite towards Speech House and Cinderford. After 50 yds near a bus shelter, turn off right along a cycleway. Follow the path for 300 yds to a junction **A**, there going left back to the car park. At the final junction, you may first wish to continue a little farther ahead to the New Fancy colliery screen where the coal was washed and loaded onto waiting railway wagons. ●

Newent and Acorn Wood

Start	Newent
Distance	5 miles (8km)
Height gain	360 feet (110m)
Approximate time	2½ hours
Parking	Town centre car park
Route terrain	Field paths, street and quiet lane
Ordnance Survey maps	Landranger 162 (Gloucester & Forest of Dean), Explorer OL14 (Wye Valley & Forest of Dean)

GPS waypoints

✏ SO 721 259
🅐 SO 713 256
🅑 SO 710 251
🅒 SO 699 237
🅓 SO 709 243
🅔 SO 720 254

Newent lies on the fringe of the Forest of Dean and from Roman times grew in importance as both a centre for iron making and a market. The surrounding countryside is noted for its profusion of wild spring daffodils, but as this walk to nearby Acorn Wood demonstrates, the undulating countryside is beautiful all year.

With many of its streets overlooked by 18th-century house fronts, an ancient church and a half-timbered market hall at its centre, Newent remains an attractive town. Few traces of its industrial past remain, which over time have included glass making, the production of cloth and coal mining.

✏ Come out of the car park opposite the library and turn right along High Street. Reaching the traffic lights, go left with the B4221 for ¼ mile. Just past the entrance to Glebe Infant School, fork off left into Bradfords Lane, going left again at the end along a narrow lane.

After a further ¼ mile, bear off right in front of the entrance to the Broadford Meadows Arboretum car park 🅐 along a track beside a thatched cottage. Through a gate, keep ahead past Elmcroft Tree Nursery on a contained path beside the house. Beyond a kissing-gate at the end, continue on a hedged gravel track to meet a lane.

Turn left, but after 250 yds leave right onto a track 🅑, which rises over the crest of a hill to Knappers Farm. Stay ahead past the farmhouse and go through a gate. Veer right to a second gate and walk beside a barn to its corner. Now bear left across the field, aiming for a sprawling oak on the far boundary. There swing right for a few yards beside an unruly hedge to an opening. Pass into the right-hand one of the two fields to walk away with a hedge on your left towards Acorn Wood.

At the top corner of the field, go through the leftmost of the two gates into the corner of the wood, but before walking on, pause to look back across the serene countryside to the Malvern Hills. Follow the path into the wood, taking the right branch where it then forks. A clear path climbs gently through the trees, emerging at the top of the hill onto a drive. Follow it ahead past sheds and a house to leave through a kissing-gate onto a lane 🅒.

Turn left past the house to the end of the lane, continuing along a descending hedged grass track. Coming out onto a

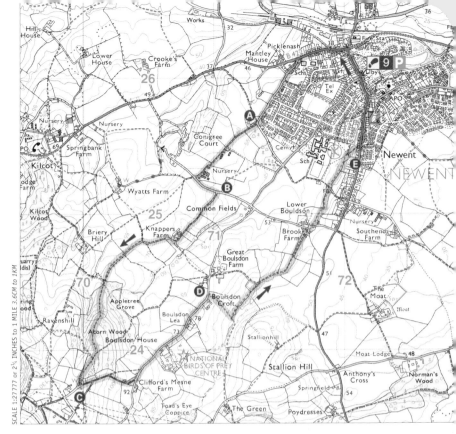

lane, go left, shortly passing the National Birds of Prey Centre. Carry on for another 600 yds before abandoning the lane on a bend through a kissing-gate beside the entrance to Boulsdon Croft Lodge **D**.

Follow the paddock boundary to a ranch stile, crossing to continue at the edge of a garden past a swimming pool. Through a gate at the bottom corner, head down a contained path between more paddocks towards a wood. There, go left on a rough grass path at the edge of the trees.

Through a kissing-gate, advance along the perimeter of the field and then past a small pond, dropping beyond to another kissing-gate. Go forward a few yards and then turn right through yet another kissing-gate. Amble on at the field's lower edge, leaving at the corner to continue on a tree-tunnelled path. Breaking into the open, carry on to a track that leads out past a farmhouse to a junction of lanes.

Bear right across a grass triangle, climbing the bank opposite to a kissing-gate. Walk away at the right-hand edge of a paddock, passing through a gate at the far end to continue on a grass path parallelling a meandering wooded stream. When you shortly reach a bridge, instead of crossing, take the uphill gravel path to the left. Through a kissing-gate at the top, turn back down to the stream and follow it as before. As houses then shortly become visible ahead, watch for a right fork that leads to a bridge over the stream **E**. Climb beyond out to a road, which, to the left takes you to the town. At the end, go left along High Street to get back to the car park. ●

King's Caple, Sellack and Hoarwithy

King's Caple, Sellack and Hoarwithy

Start	King's Caple	**GPS waypoints**	
Distance	5 miles (8km)	🥾	SO 559 288
Height gain	375 feet (115m)	**Ⓐ**	SO 564 289
		Ⓑ	SO 564 281
Approximate time	2½ hours	**Ⓒ**	SO 565 276
Parking	Roadside parking by church	**Ⓓ**	SO 550 277
		Ⓔ	SO 542 275
Route terrain	Field paths and quiet lanes	**Ⓕ**	SO 549 294
Ordnance Survey maps	Landrangers 149 (Hereford & Leominster) and 162 (Gloucester & Forest of Dean), Explorer 189 (Hereford & Ross-on-Wye)		

Snaking lazily amid low hills, the Wye Valley between Hereford and Ross is something of a contrast to the gorge farther downstream. The landscape is patterned with a mélange of meadows, fields, orchards and woodland clumps, criss-crossed by narrow lanes and old trackways linking hamlets and farmsteads. This walk revels in the scenery and links three tiny villages, each with a quite different church.

King's Caple is an ancient settlement, with a Norman motte, Caple Tump, and a road that was originally Roman lying opposite the church. The oldest parts of the church date from the 13th century, but like most ecclesiastical buildings, it has been remodelled and extended over the centuries. Inside are box pews installed in 1638 and a high pulpit crowned by a sounding board dating from the same period. The stepped cross in the churchyard has long been known as the 'Plague Cross', but it was only in the 1970s when repairs to the path were being undertaken that a plague pit was discovered. It contained over 25 bodies, people thought to have perished during the Black Death of 1348. As the plague swept unchecked across the country, few areas escaped and more than one third of the terrified population perished.

🥾 From the church follow the lane east, going straight over a crossroads by the old village school. Carry on past the modern school and then Caple Avenue, leaving just beyond along a track on the right beside High House **Ⓐ**. Where it divides, take the left branch, going through a couple of gates at the end into a field. Walk on ahead, joining a hedge on your left, which leads to a stile in the corner.

Climbing over, there is a view to your next objective, the 14th-century spire of Sellack's sandstone church. Head towards it on a cleared path through a crop field, later accompanying a hedge on your right. Where that subsequently turns away, keep going forward to the bottom of the field, exiting over a stile onto a narrow lane.

Turn right, walking down past

cottages to a sharp right-hand bend **B**. Leave left through a gate along a waymarked path shaded by an outgrown hedge and which leads to a suspension bridge across the River Wye. The supports for the bridge were cast in Aberdeen and the span erected in 1895 to replace a ferry that operated from the northern bank. On the far bank, keep straight ahead across the meadows and an intervening footbridge, making for a stile by the church **C**.

The church is dedicated to a 7th-century Welsh saint, Tysilio, a prince by birth but who turned his back upon the court to become a hermit monk and ended up a bishop. Like the churches at Hoarwithy and King's Caple it honours the custom of giving pax cakes at the conclusion of the Palm Sunday service. The practice dates back to 1484, when the vicar, Thomas More bequeathed 6s 8d 'for bread and ale ... to be distributed to all and singular in

the aforesaid churches for the good of my soul'.

Return over the stile and now go left to a second stile. Head away on a trod along an expansive meadow at a fine angle from the woodland bank to your left. Eventually closing with the river, follow it upstream, a track eventually developing beyond a gate. Stay with the track as it later swings away from the river to a junction of lanes **D**.

Take the one opposite to Kynaston and Hentland, following it uphill for ½ mile to a sharp bend **E**. Leave along a waymarked track on the right, but where that then swings left by a pylon, keep ahead on a hedge-tunnelled, sunken path. Over a stile beside a gate at the end, carry on beside the top hedge continuing in a second field. Mount a stile towards the far end of the

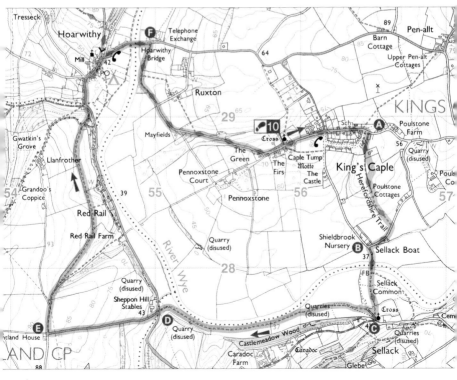

fence, crossing a grass track into the field opposite. Walk on by the left hedge, dropping through a clump of trees at the far side to emerge onto a track.

Go right and immediately left beside a cottage, Quarry Bank and follow another old banked path. Coming out onto a lane at the bottom, turn left into Hoarwithy. Keep ahead at a junction past the **New Harp Inn**, where in the garden over to the left is an apple press.

The church with its striking belvedere tower stands on a low hill overlooking the village. To reach it, walk past the next junction and almost immediately turn up a flight of steps on the left.

Come here on a balmy summer's day and you might think you were in Umbria. The church is the creation of William Poole, who came as vicar to neighbouring Hentland in 1854. He disliked the plain edifice erected by his predecessor and on inheriting his family's fortune commissioned J P Seddon, a noted Victorian church architect to design something more pleasing. Inspired by the religious architecture of France and Italy, the work was painstaking and took over 20 years to complete. The building was finally dedicated in 1904.

Return to the junction and go left towards King's Caple. Walk down past a second junction to Hoarwithy Bridge, overseen by a cottage built for the toll collector. The first bridge, built of wood to replace the ancient ferry, was erected in 1856. However, after only 20 years it was succeeded by one made of iron, which remained in use until 1990.

On the far bank ⓕ, turn right on a path that briefly joins the river before turning away to rise to the bend of a lane. Walk ahead, climbing a gentle hill, later keeping left at a junction to return to King's Caple. ●

The Wye Valley near King's Caple

Sugar Loaf

Start	Sugar Loaf car park on Llanwenarth Hill, 2½ miles north west of Abergavenny and accessed along narrow lanes from A40	**GPS waypoints** ⬛ SO 268 167 Ⓐ SO 272 187 Ⓑ SO 287 162 Ⓒ SO 278 167 Ⓓ SO 275 162 Ⓔ SO 270 168
Distance	5½ miles (8.9km)	
Height gain	1,475 feet (450m)	
Approximate time	3 hours	
Parking	Car park at start	
Route terrain	Hill and woodland paths, some quiet lanes	
Ordnance Survey maps	Landranger 161 (The Black Mountains), Explorer OL13 (Brecon Beacons National Park – Eastern area)	

Although less dramatic than its namesake overlooking Rio de Janeiro in Brazil, Abergavenny's Sugar Loaf is an appealing hill and its summit ascent is deservedly one of the area's most popular walks. It is an outlier of the Black Mountains and its relative isolation from the surrounding hills endows it with superb views in every direction. Despite a height approaching 2,000 feet, the climb is relatively undemanding, the return taking a leisurely line along the south-western shoulder of Rholben and curving into the beautiful wooded valley of St Mary's Vale.

In poor visibility, the hill's confusing array of paths may cause navigation difficulties for inexperienced walkers.

⬛ Leave the car park along the path slanting left uphill from the information board across the common above Llyweddrog Farm, the top of the hill soon coming into view. Reaching the corner of a wall take the left fork and then at the next corner branch right. Keep ahead over a crosspath, the way briefly descending to reveal the onward route. At the next crossing, go left, the path soon curving right and passing another junction as it fixes its line towards the summit. Beyond another crossing the way continues steadily upwards, ultimately raking right for the

final pull to the top Ⓐ.

For such a rounded mountain the top is surprisingly impressive, a short ridge that gives stunning 360-degree views. The ground falls on all sides to lush valleys while in the distance to the west are the Brecon Beacons and far to the south beyond Abergavenny is the mouth of the River Severn. The town below stands on the site of a Roman fort, the area already then important for the smelting of iron. The town's name derived from the old Welsh Gobannia – River of Blacksmiths.

The way off lies over to the right, the initial abruptness shortly ameliorating into a steady descent towards the south east. Soon picking up the course of a sparkling spring, cross it lower down. Reaching a diagonal crosspath, keep ahead and then just beyond, bear left at a fork. The path settles beside an old boundary bank, thick with bilberry, which is later replaced by a broken wall and fence. At the end of the fence, remain ahead where the path divides, soon dropping to a gate off the hill. Pass

through a clump of trees to a lane **B**.

Turn right, following the lane through a gate to a junction and go right again. Now gently climbing, bear left at a fork by a small parking area. Continue beyond a house and through a gate along a woodland track. An old clapper bridge takes you dry-footed across a stream, but higher up, after heavy rain, it can escape its normal flow to spill over the track. Follow the

On top of Sugar Loaf

SCALE 1:25 000 or 2½ INCHES to 1 MILE 4CM to 1KM

0	200	400	600	800 METRES	1
KILOMETRES
MILES

| 0 | 200 | 400 | 600 YARDS | ½ |

track on through the woodland of St Mary's Vale, one of the most delightful stretches of the walk.

Eventually the track doubles back left **C** to gain height along the valley side, later leaving the wood and rising as a gravel track to a lane. Go right and bear right, the way signed back to the car park. However, rather than simply follow the lane, you can take a path back onto the hill. It leaves after ¼ mile, just before a National Trust boundary marker and passing place **D**, climbing off sharp right through the bracken.

Farther up curve left and then go forward over a crossing. The path then fragments, but keep walking ahead, all the time making for the highest ground. Eventually the gradient eases and the path settles along the broad spine of the hill, with Sugar Loaf once more to be seen in all its glory overlooking the head of St Mary's Vale. Carry on for another 400 yds and then take the third clear path off on the left **E**. Head down the slope back to the car park, which soon appears below.

Mordiford and Haugh Wood

		GPS waypoints	
Start	Mordiford	✔	SO 567 375
Distance	6 miles (9.7km)	**A**	SO 570 374
Height gain	590 feet (180m)	**B**	SO 581 351
Approximate time	3 hours	**C**	SO 589 351
Parking	Roadside parking west of Mordiford Bridge	**D**	SO 592 365
		E	SO 588 378
Route terrain	Field paths and forest tracks		
Ordnance Survey maps	Landranger 149 (Hereford & Leominster), Explorer 189 (Hereford & Ross-on-Wye)		

Beginning from the medieval Mordiford Bridge, said to be the oldest surviving in Herefordshire, the route follows the Wye Valley Walk to return by way of Haugh Wood. Once belonging to Hereford Cathedral, it is now managed by the Forestry Commission and is an important butterfly reserve.

Walk over the bridge into the tiny village, following the road past Holy Rood Church. Just beyond, go right beside the post office **A**, crossing a brook to turn left beside the stream. Re-emerging onto the road, cross to the yard opposite, walking past the old mill into a small field.

A track takes the way over a brook into the next field. Keep going by the boundary to a kissing-gate in the corner, through which go over another stream. Bear away to walk with a hedge on your right at the edge of a large orchard, leaving through a gate along a contained track to cottages. Keep ahead down a lane to a junction by converted barns at Hope Springs.

Turning right, pass between them and on beside a sprawling working barn, a farm track meandering beyond across the fields. Keep with the main track at a fork near a cottage, the way gently falling along a wide, pleasant valley bordered by wooded hills.

Entering a large field through a gate, carry on ahead, joining a line of trees and hedge on your left towards the far side. The grass track descends into the narrowing point of the field dropping beyond through a gate to a junction of tracks. Walk ahead and curve left over a bridge onto a lane **B**.

Go left for some ½ mile, eventually reaching a field gate on the right before a small bridge. Across the field, an apple press forms a monument to Tom Spring, one-time All England Bare Knuckle Champion.

Continue along the lane to a cottage, turning left just beyond onto a track **C**. Walk for 200 yds to find a broad path climbing past a barrier into the wood. Higher up, join a track to a junction beside a bench and a butterfly information panel.

An ongoing process of conifer thinning and native planting is changing the character of the wood to favour the butterflies and moths for

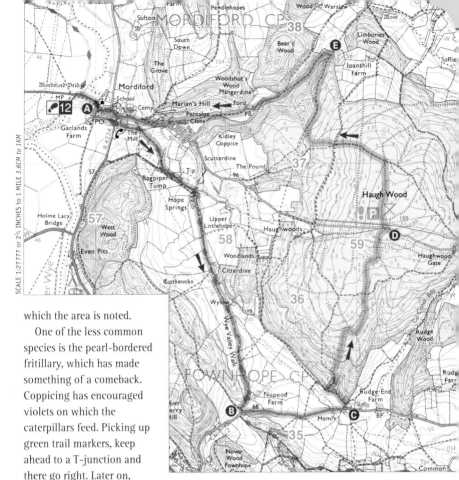

which the area is noted.

One of the less common species is the pearl-bordered fritillary, which has made something of a comeback. Coppicing has encouraged violets on which the caterpillars feed. Picking up green trail markers, keep ahead to a T-junction and there go right. Later on, reaching another T-junction walk left, ultimately leaving the wood past a barrier onto a lane opposite a car park **D**.

Cross and take the track opposite past the car park and beside a barrier into the northern part of the forest, initially following a red waymarked trail. At a junction turn left, but then at a crossroads, keep ahead to leave the butterfly trail. Ignoring side paths the way descends the hill, later dropping through a hairpin **E** and subsequently reaching a junction.

Go left, initially beside a stream, but after some 250 yds, look for a path marked off to the right, which loses height to a gate at the edge of the forest. Walk on at the perimeter of a flower meadow past the sadly decaying ruin of a small wattle and daub cottage.

Joining a track bear left, but as it then passes into a second meadow, fork right off the track, crossing the pasture to close alongside more woodland.

Leave at the corner behind houses through a kissing-gate, from which a path leads out to a street. Go right to the end and look for a narrow path in the trees skirting left of a small substation. It runs behind more houses to emerge onto a lane. Walk right towards Mordiford.

At a junction with the main road by the **Moon Inn**, go right and follow it back through the village, passing the church and crossing the bridge to the starting point.

●

Ruardean and Astonbridgehill Inclosure

Start	Cannop Valley Speculation, off B4234 ¾ mile south of A4136
Distance	6 miles (9.7km)
Height gain	705 feet (215m)
Approximate time	3 hours
Parking	Car park at start
Route terrain	Forest paths and tracks
Ordnance Survey maps	Landranger 162 (Gloucester & Forest of Dean), Explorer OL14 (Wye Valley & Forest of Dean)

GPS waypoints

- ✒ SO 613 136
- Ⓐ SO 616 143
- Ⓑ SO 624 151
- Ⓒ SO 623 164
- Ⓓ SO 620 173
- Ⓔ SO 614 168
- Ⓕ SO 609 164
- Ⓖ SO 607 159
- Ⓗ SO 615 147

Ruardean was once an industrialised community, with mines, forges and quarries providing noisy and dirty employment that spilled into the surrounding forest. Streams powered mills and wood was cut for charcoal, while 19th-century railway lines, bridges and tunnels replaced the traditional packhorse and cart trails. Since the mines and quarries have closed, nature has healed many of the scars and it now often needs a knowing eye to spot the relics of industry.

✒ From a post marking the Speculation Forest Trail at the rear of the car park, walk up to a junction by a signpost and take the broad track to the left, not the narrower cycle path. After ½ mile, keep ahead at a crossing Ⓐ, continuing until you eventually reach a T-junction. Go left and carry on through the forest for another ½ mile before passing through a barrier to meet a forest road. Turn left out to the main road at Brierley.

Cross and turn right, walking down to the first lane leaving on the left and signed to The Pludds Ⓑ. It takes the route into a quiet valley, once shared with the railway. After ½ mile, cross a small bridge and go off right along a broad forest track into a side fold, Ware Slade. As the main track then shortly swings over a bridge, fork left on a path climbing above the stream. Ultimately passing through a barrier, leave the trees and continue across the slope of a clearing to meet the sharp bend of a lane Ⓒ.

Still climbing, take the left branch, which opens a view across the valley to the former colliery settlement of Ruardean Woodside. However, all that betrays its former industry is a heap of spoil, now softened by vegetation, at the northern end of the settlement. At the top of the lane, follow a footpath straight ahead over a stile. Walk on at the field edge, passing in the second field a small spoil heap, one of several dotting the open rolling hillside. Leaving over a stone

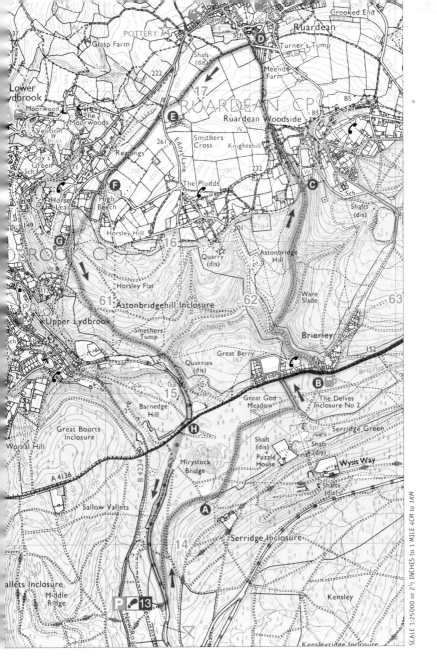

SCALE 1:25 000 or 2½ INCHES to 1 MILE 4CM to 1KM

stile, go forward to join a contained path, which emerges at the junction of Pettycroft and Kingsway lanes above the village of Ruardean **D**. The spot is a grand viewpoint to the distant Malvern Hills, while closer to is the slender spire of St John the Baptist's Church.

Until the middle of the 20th century, Ruardean was an industrial village, with iron smelting, nail making and coal mining all major activities. It has another claim to fame too, for born in the village were James and William Horlick, sons of the local vicar. They subsequently emigrated to America and

Ruardean and the Wye Valley from Ruardean Hill

set up a factory to produce a malted milk drink they had devised as a food for infants. However, it soon attracted a wider market and *Horlicks* became a household name, being taken by explorers to both poles and issued to troops during two world wars.

Take the hedge-tunnelled path leaving over to the left between two gates. At its end, cross a stile and continue at the field edge from where you can gaze out across the heart of the forest. Partway along beside an old boundary stone, the path slips through the hedge to the other flank, swapping the views for the Black Mountains of Wales. Over a stile in the corner, bear right on a trod across a flower-rich meadow to emerge onto a lane **E**.

Go left past a viewpoint, where a topograph can help locate the features of the wider countryside. Just beyond, bear right onto a woodland track, which climbs over a low rise to come out at a junction of lanes. Take the left branch, but after 70 yds at a bend, leave ahead on a gently descending grass track **F**. Reaching a junction, take the gravel track opposite. Where that then turns into the yard of a house, again keep forward on a grass path. A few paces farther on, approaching a small ivy-clad stone building, bear off right into

woodland. As you pass under power cables running through a cleared swathe, turn right onto a narrower path that drops to a lane.

Follow it down to a sharp bend, there abandoning the lane for a forest path ahead **G**. Keep with it as it meanders easily downhill for ½ mile and then drops more steeply to a T-junction above a deep wooded fold. Go left and immediately right to cross a culverted stream. Some 300 yds farther on, swing through a gap in the right-hand embankment onto a broad track. Follow it left over a bridge and then take the right branch at a fork, climbing steeply through hairpins and above a deep cutting before turning away to meet the main road **H**.

Cross to the continuing path opposite, remaining with it as it veers right past a junction. A short way along, over to the left, is the southern portal of the Mirystock Tunnel, while a little farther on is the Mirystock Bridge. They are both relics of the Severn and Wye Railway, whose network of tracks connected mines and quarries within the forest and eventually crossed the River Severn to Sharpness. The first section between Lydney and Lydbrook opened in 1810 as a horse-drawn tramway and was later converted to steam with extensions added to Coleford and Cinderford. It declined during the 20th century, first losing passenger services and later being closed in sections as mines and quarries ceased production. It finally finished in 1976, although a short section between Lydney and Parkend has been restored as the Dean Forest Railway. Carry on along the path for another ¾ mile back to the car park. ●

Bredwardine, Arthur's Stone and Merbach Hill

Start	Bredwardine	**GPS waypoints**	
Distance	6 miles (9.7km)	🖉 SO 334 445	
Height gain	855 feet (260m)	Ⓐ SO 338 432	
		Ⓑ SO 328 426	
Approximate time	3 hours	Ⓒ SO 318 431	
Parking	Verges along lane leading to church at Bredwardine	Ⓓ SO 303 447	
		Ⓔ SO 325 443	
Route terrain	Country lanes, field paths and tracks		
Ordnance Survey maps	Landranger 148 (Presteigne & Hay-on-Wye), Explorer OL13 (Brecon Beacons National Park – Eastern area)		

Merbach Hill and its associated ridge separate the Golden Valley from that of the River Wye and offer a grand but relatively undemanding walk that looks across to the northern fringe of the Black Mountains. Beginning from Bredwardine, with its pretty church and early castle earthworks it climbs onto the ridge where there is a Neolithic burial chamber. The open common of Merbach Hill is rich in wildlife from which the route makes a leisurely descent back to the river.

King Arthur's Stone

St Andrew's Church clearly incorporates work of many periods, the earliest portions perhaps dating to Saxon times. Of special interest is the herringbone masonry of the north wall and the carved lintels over the south and (now blocked) north doors. That in the porch carries a geometric design while the one in the north wall incorporates figures of what appears to be a bird and a grotesque, possibly a sheela na gig, an ancient fertility symbol.

The Victorian diarist Francis Kilvert spent the last two years of his life as vicar here before his untimely death in 1879 from peritonitis, a few days after returning from honeymoon. Kilvert's diaries were never intended for publication but his inquisitive eye for detail and appealing style captured the essence of this rural border country. Following his death, much was lost but selections of what remains have been variously published and a television dramatisation was produced in the 1970s. His grave can be seen in the churchyard behind the tower.

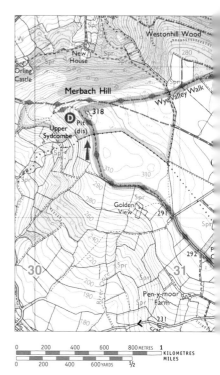

🔁 Facing the church, take the bridleway to the right, which soon narrows to a hollow path. Weaving through trees, the way shortly descends to a reedy pond and is carried over its marshy head on a boardwalk. Keep going past a wooded mound, thought to be the site of an early castle and then pass through a gap to cross a stream. Bear right over a hillock to a gate and follow a track to the right, which shortly leads out to a lane.

Walk left for ¼ mile before turning right along a track to Bodcott Farm **Ⓐ**. Reaching the yard, pass between the buildings to a gate, right of the farmhouse. Of the three gates immediately beyond, pass through that on the left and climb away along a hedged, green lane. Eventually emerging into a field at the top, there is the first of many views across the Wye Valley. Keep going by the left edge, soon picking up the track once more, which leads out to a lane.

Turn up the hill, going right at a junction near the top **Ⓑ** onto a narrow lane, signed to Arthur's Stone. Beyond another sharp pull the way settles along the broad ridge between the Wye and Golden valleys. Half a mile's walking takes you to Arthur's Stone **Ⓒ**.

One of innumerable monuments scattered around the country attributed to the legendary king, it is in fact a Neolithic chambered tomb dating from between 3,700 to 2,700BC, perhaps 1,000 years older than the Great Pyramid of Giza. Originally covered by a long

mound of earth, the central chamber was entered from the west along an 'L' shaped passage. Conspicuously sited on the hill, it would have served as a focal point for the tribe; a place to gather for seasonal ceremonies as well as for the burial of the dead and perhaps veneration of ancestors.

Continue along the straight ridge-top lane for a further ¾ mile to a sharp, right-hand bend by a cottage. Walk forward through a gate along a gravel track, keeping ahead beside an outgrown hedge when it then swings left. As the ground later begins to fall away, bear right maintaining the edge of the high ground to a gate onto Merbach Hill Common. A path leads on across the bracken heath, winding between the hollows of old workings to a triangulation pillar **Ⓓ**.

Both sandstone and limestone were quarried around the summit, the latter burned in nearby kilns to produce lime.

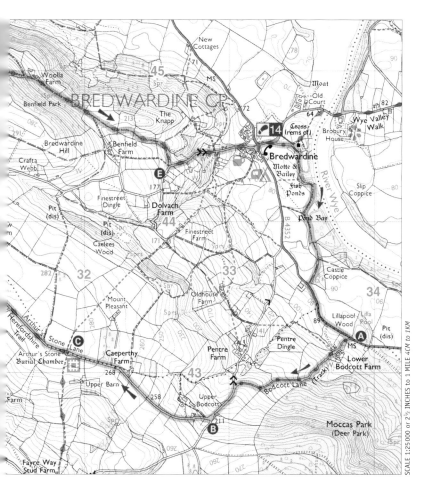

SCALE 1:25 000 or 2½ INCHES to 1 MILE 4CM to 1KM

The flower-rich grassland is now an important habitat for ground nesting birds such as the meadow pipit and skylark.

To the right, a path falls east through scrub woodland, eventually leading to a gate at the edge of the common. Keep ahead across a meadow to another gate in the corner. Carry on at the field boundary and then along a short enclosed track, resuming with the field edge to pass a tumbled-down barn. Beyond the gate there, bear right through another gate to continue downhill on a track to Woolla Farm.

Abandon the track at the farm gate, leaving through a small wooden gate just to the right for a path into a wood.

Skirt around the farm, rejoining the track at the far side. After crossing a cattle-grid, walk on for another 100 yds to the second telegraph post, there striking off left across a grassy slope. Keep going through a waymarked gap in an old hedge line and bear right to a small gate in the far bottom corner. Go a short distance farther along the bottom of the next field and then turn right through a gate to accompany a track out to a lane **E**.

Follow the lane steeply downhill to a crossroads by the **Red Lion Hotel** and carry on along the lane opposite past a slender stone cross, the village war memorial. Fork off right to go back to the church. ●

Tintern Abbey and the Devil's Pulpit

Start	Tintern	**GPS waypoints**	
Distance	6 miles (9.7km)	◢ SO 528 005	
Height gain	985 feet (300m)	Ⓐ SO 529 002	
		Ⓑ ST 540 982	
Approximate time	3 hours	Ⓒ ST 541 987	
Parking	Roadside parking areas at Tintern	Ⓓ SO 545 013	
Route terrain	Woodland paths and tracks	Ⓔ SO 539 011	
Ordnance Survey maps	Landranger 162 (Gloucester & Forest of Dean), Explorer OL14 (Wye Valley & Forest of Dean)		

Tintern is one of the most impressive ruinous abbeys in the country, for the walls of the great church remain intact, rising to their full height and pierced by soaring windows that flooded the interior with light. It lies beside this walk of spectacular views, which follows the Wye gorge downstream before climbing to return above the valley along Offa's Dyke. Passed along the way is the Devil's Pulpit, a rocky outcrop overlooking the abbey far below.

📷 Follow the main road south into the village, passing a second parking area before reaching a junction beside Abbey Mill Ⓐ. The entrance to the abbey lies a little farther along the road.

Founded in 1131 by Walter de Clare, the Lord of Chepstow, the abbey was the first Cistercian house in Wales. But although generously endowed, something that financed significant rebuilding throughout its life, the monastery never grew to great importance. Like the other monastic communities of England and Wales, the abbot, monks and lay workers were evicted under Henry VIII's Dissolution of the monasteries and it has stood empty since 1536. Although stripped of its roof, lead and glass and quarried for building stone, the abbey remains remarkably complete. A 'tourist attraction' since the 18th century, it has

inspired artists and writers, including Turner, Gilpin and Wordsworth and continues to attract visitors to this lovely corner of Wales.

Return to Abbey Mill Ⓐ and turn to the river, crossing a bridge from which there is a picture to the abbey. At a junction on the far bank, take the track to the right. Some 150 yds along, you can optionally drop through a kissing-gate into the meadow below and follow a riverside path for a view of the abbey. Return to the main track as it then joins the line of the former Wye Valley Railway, which emerges from a short tunnel piercing the high headland that forced a tight bend in the river. The bordering trees largely obscure sight of the Wye as the track imperceptibly gains height in its course along the valley. Farther on it gently curves away, emerging from the trees to a fork. Branch left, rising to a junction with a broad forest track **B** and go sharp left, climbing more steeply to a second junction.

Opposite to the right, a narrow path rises enthusiastically through the dense wood. Meeting a crossing path turn right, but after a few yards, go left to resume the upward pull. At the top, it broaches the defensive ditch and embankment of Offa's Dyke **C**. One of the great Anglo-Saxon kings, Offa ruled Mercia from 757 to 796. The dyke marked the western limit of his kingdom and ran for 150 miles from the River Dee to the River Severn.

Turn left, gently weaving through the trees above the steep bank of Shorn Cliff. Later, at the crest, ignore the path off right, descending beyond to a partial clearing where the trees straddling the earthwork have been felled. Below to the left is a free standing pillar of rock,

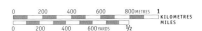

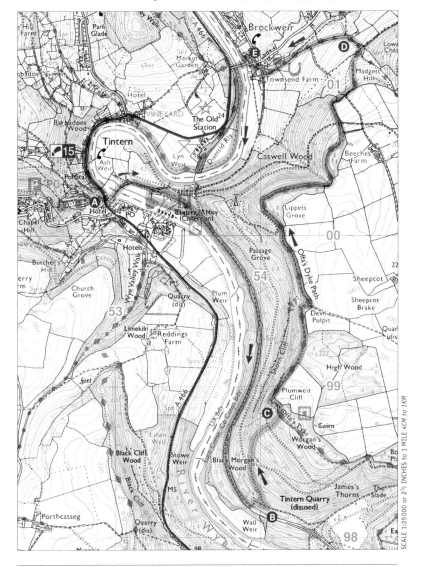

the Devil's Pulpit. It offers a superb view past the abbey and is so named because the Devil supposedly appeared here to entice the monks from their devotions.

Carry on along the dyke, shortly reaching a three-way signpost. Swing down left towards Tintern, Brockweir and St Briavels, but at the next junction, keep ahead with Offa's Dyke to Brockweir and St Briavels. The path eventually falls to a crossing of tracks. Go straight ahead over a stile, passing several burrows of a large badger sett at the edge of the wood. Setts can remain in use over many generations and badgers have obviously been a feature here for a long time, hence the name of the village below, Brockweir.

Watch for a waypost guiding you left at a fork, dropping from the trees into a sloping meadow. Head downfield to a stile at the bottom right corner and continue along an old tree-lined way to a signpost **D**. Take the left branch of the Offa's Dyke Path to Brockweir, following a field track down the hillside to Gregory Farm, a horse rescue centre. Walk past the stables and at the bottom go right, emerging in the village at the foot of Mill Hill by the **Brockweir Country Inn E**.

Follow the lane left over the River Wye, but then immediately abandon it down steps on the left, the way signed to Tintern. At the bottom you can either bear left to take a riverside path or alternatively keep straight ahead, following the course of the Wye Valley Railway to the Old Station, where there is a **café** in the restored waiting room. Carry on through to the end of the narrow gauge railway line, where the path drops to the right off the embankment to join the riverside path below the abutment of a dismantled bridge that used to take the railway across the river. Through a gate the path continues around a bend of the river, ultimately leading into the little churchyard of St Michael at Tintern Parva.

Passing through the churchyard, walk ahead on a short back lane that leads out to the main road. Go left back to the car park. ●

Tintern Abbey, with the wooded slopes of the Forest of Dean beyond

Abbey Dore, Ewyas Harold and the Dulas Valley

		GPS waypoints
Start	Abbey Dore	📷 SO 386 303
Distance	6¼ miles (10.1km)	**A** SO 385 298
Height gain	870 feet (265m)	**B** SO 388 287
Approximate time	3 hours	**C** SO 372 289
Parking	Roadside parking by Dore Abbey	**D** SO 369 294
Route terrain	Field paths	**E** SO 381 299
Dog friendly	2 stepped high stiles	**F** SO 380 305
Ordnance Survey maps	Landranger 161 (The Black Mountains), Explorer OL13 (Brecon Beacons National Park – Eastern area)	**G** SO 388 309

The beautiful Golden Valley encloses a tributary stream of the River Wye and its seclusion drew Cistercian monks to settle there in the 12th century. The walk begins from the site of the abbey, crossing an ancient common to nearby Ewyas Harold. The return is by a roundabout route above the neighbouring Dulas Valley that offers fine panoramas across the Welsh Borders.

It was the Normans who called the valley golden, misinterpreting the Welsh dŵr as their own word d'or. The name stuck and is not inappropriate, for wild flowers, ripening hay and corn and autumnal leaves each contribute to golden tints throughout the year. To the monks who built the abbey, the valley must have indeed seemed golden, for the foundation was endowed with extensive tracts of fertile land. The community flourished, enabling the construction of a great church. After the Dissolution, the domestic buildings and much of the church was pulled down, the stone taken for use elsewhere. But part of the church was left standing and gives some idea of the scale and fine craftsmanship of the original building. Following conservation and repairs in the 1990s it remains the local church

and is a regular venue for concerts and recitals.

📷 The walk begins over a stile directly opposite the lychgate to the abbey church. Bear left to the top corner of the field, cross a stile hidden in the trees and maintain your diagonal across a paddock towards a cottage. Ignore the stile there and instead swing right through a gap into the field above. Climb beside the boundary to a stile below another cottage. A contained path winds around its perimeter, emerging onto the edge of Ewyas Harold Common. Walk forward across a concrete track and bear left, joining a grass swathe to a crossing of grass paths **A**.

Turn left and then curve right in front of a shingle-clad cottage to follow a broad swathe that gently descends across the common. Ahead, the view is to Garway Hill, but closer to, you are likely to encounter grazing ponies.

Eventually you come upon a gravel track by a cottage. Follow it down, merging with another track to reach a junction. Go right but then almost immediately bear off right again onto a broad path descending through bracken. Passing into trees, swing left at the bottom onto another path, which rises to a stile. Head down across a sloping pasture, keeping left of a line of hazel to find a stile tucked in the bottom corner. Continue down the next field, emerging onto a junction of streets at the edge of Ewyas Harold **B**. Take the street ahead, which leads into the centre of the village beside the **Temple Bar Inn**.

Turn right, passing the **Dog Inn** and follow the lane out of the village. After some 200 yds, as it bends right, climb to a gate on the left. A stepped path rises through a tangled corner of wood to come out at the edge of a meadow, dominated by the mound of an early Norman castle. Head out, passing left of the hillock and joining a track leading to farm buildings.

Follow it between the sheds and pass through a gate at the far side into a field. Walk along its edge to a shallow corner and go through the leftmost of the two gates. Carry on, the hedge now on your right, ignoring a stile partway along the second field. Beyond a gate in the corner, keep going, the hedge once more on your left.

Over a stile, cross the next pasture to its far-right corner by a wood, passing through a gap into the next field. Pick up a trod that diverges from the trees, aiming for a metal gate that soon comes into view beside an indented corner. Pass it to the left, continuing into the corner of the large field **C**. Amble on at the edge of the subsequent pastures, occasional gaps in the hedge giving a

view towards Hay Bluff.

Leave through a gate at Plash farm. Bearing right, skirt the garden in front of the farmhouse and then turn left beside a barn. By the barn's rear corner, go over a stile on the right into a rough area. Walk down a few yards and go right again over another stile into a field behind the farmhouse. Striking half-left, walk diagonally downfield, maintaining the same direction in a second field to find a stile hidden in trees at the far bottom-right corner.

Entering a wood, descend through the trees, bearing left and dropping to a stile. Carry on to exit the wood over a second stile, continuing down the edge of open pasture and finally leaving at the bottom onto a lane **D**.

To the right, it leads past a small church to a junction. Double back left along a drive to Dulas Court, now operated as a residential care home for the elderly. Keep to the main drive, swinging right at the far end around a group of bungalows and on across a bridge over Dulas Brook. Just after, and before reaching a cottage, turn off right along the edge of a small orchard to a stile and gate. Walk into the field and bear left, gaining height to a stile in the top corner.

Go right on a grassy uphill track through trees, keeping right at a junction and then at a fork just beyond. A few yards farther on, however, look for a waymark indicating a narrow path off on the left. Climb to the top of the wood and leave over a stile. Strike across a rough pasture to a stile in the upper right-hand corner and walk on towards Cot Farm. Wind left and right between the barns into another field and carry on along its top edge. Over a stile at the far side, head on down to a final stile at the edge of Ewyas Harold Common **E**.

Walk forward on a broad grass swathe to the sharp bend of a gravel track. Bear right on the gently descending lower branch. Where that subsequently swings sharply right, keep ahead on a falling grassy path. Reaching an intersection, go left a short distance to reach another crossing **Ⓐ** and turn left again.

You might simply retrace your outward steps to the abbey church, the path you came up being over to the right. Otherwise carry on ahead, crossing a turning circle towards a cottage, to the left of which is a waymarked field gate. Walk away beside the field's upper boundary, from which there is a picturesque view across Golden Valley.

In the corner, climb a high but sturdy ladder-stile over a deer fence and maintain your line across the park. Towards the far end, join a hedge on your right and walk down to another high stile. Follow a track out past Cwm Farm, but as it swings away right, watch for a waymark indicating the footpath through a gate beside a barn. Cut the corner of an old paddock to

exit through a gate onto a lane **Ⓕ**.

Turn down the hill to meet the main road and keep ahead to the next junction. Go left towards Abbey Dore Court Garden, following the lane for a little over ¼ mile. Not far beyond the entrance to Abbey Dore Court, take a waymarked track on the right **Ⓖ**. Bear off right in front of a tall gate along a grass track, passing through a kissing-gate to continue beside a high perimeter fence. Winding round, the path follows the River Dore to a footbridge. Over this, head out across open grazing, aiming just left of the abbey church and cross a smaller paddock to reach the rear of the graveyard. Walk through back to the lane. ●

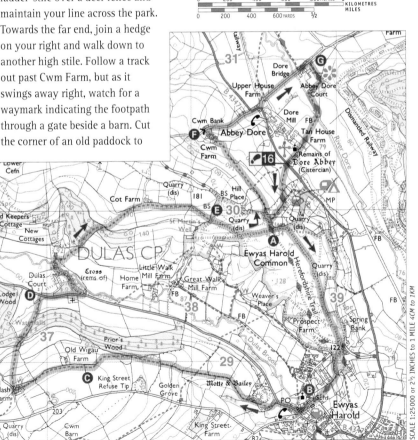

SCALE 1:25 000 or 2½ INCHES to 1 MILE 4CM to 1KM

Tidenham Chase and Wintour's Leap

		GPS waypoints
Start	Tidenham Chase	🔳 ST 558 992
Distance	6½ miles (10.5km)	**A** ST 560 985
Height gain	755 feet (230m)	**B** ST 556 972
Approximate time	3½ hours	**C** ST 556 961
Parking	Car park at start	**D** ST 551 959
Route terrain	Field paths, tracks and some lanes	**E** ST 542 961
		F ST 544 966
Ordnance Survey maps	Landranger 162 (Gloucester & Forest of Dean), Explorer OL14 (Wye Valley & Forest of Dean)	**G** ST 551 977
		H ST 551 983
		J ST 554 985
		K ST 552 990

Tidenham Chase lies at the southern edge of the forest, occupying the narrowing high ground between the Severn and the Wye. Its plantations and woodland are broken by open heath and farmland, revealing splendid panoramas across the valleys on either side. The walk courts the eastern slopes through Boughspring to Tidenham, returning above the Wye past a stunning viewpoint along a well-defined section of Offa's Dyke.

🔳 Cross the main road to a kissing-gate opposite the car park and take a path into scrub. It soon curves right onto gorse and bracken heath, intercepting a broader path. Go right, but beyond a clearing, watch for the path bearing left parallel to the south-western boundary of the heath and eventually leading to a stile out onto a lane.

Walk left, leaving after 200 yds along a waymarked track on the right into woodland **A**. Reaching a fork, bear right and then, not far beyond keep ahead over a staggered crossing, the path passing through an area where felling of conifers has opened the ground to colonisation by native deciduous trees. Paths converge to a stile at the far side of the wood. Carry on ahead at the edge of scrub. This in turn falls back to grassland, across which a trod descends to a kissing-gate. Continue downhill, crossing a stile to follow a hedge. Over another stile hidden beneath trees in the corner, head down at the perimeter of a small meadow and subsequently within a fringe of trees to emerge at a junction of lanes at Boughspring **B**.

Go left and then immediately right, passing a converted 19th-century Wesleyan Chapel. There, fork off right and walk ahead through a field gate along a narrow strip of grass. At the end cross a stile and turn right at the border of a meadow After some 30 yds watch for a stile in the accompanying hedge and climb into the adjacent field. Bear left around an indented corner to find another stile and continue at the edge

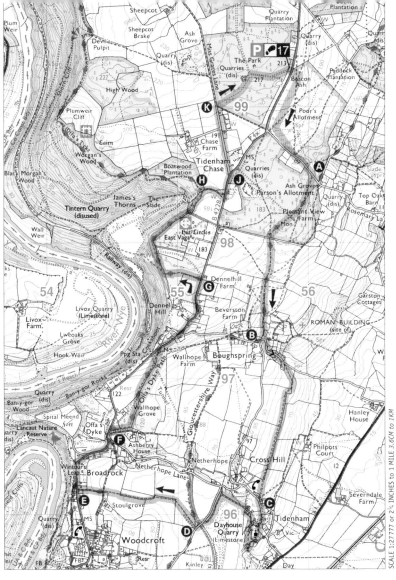

SCALE 1:27777 or 2¼ INCHES to 1 MILE 3.6CM to 1KM

0	200	400	600	800 METRES	1
					KILOMETRES
					MILES
0	200	400	600 YARDS	½	

of successive fields, eventually coming out onto a lane at the top end of Tidenham by the Old School **C**.

Stride downhill, leaving ahead at the next bend along a sunken grass path below the gardens of Tidenham Manor. Entering the expansive graveyard of Tidenham's church at the end, walk through to leave by the lychgate. Cross a stone stile over to the right and then, a few yards along, turn right through a gap. Climb a zigzagging path behind the grounds of the big house, newly built in the Georgian style on the site of the original manor. At the top, the path skirts two sides of the wooded fringe of Dayhouse Quarry to a T-junction. Go left along the third side eventually emerging onto a lane.

Walk left over a bridge spanning a disused railway line, turning off just after through a kissing-gate on the right **D**. By a sign for the Gloucestershire Way, a broad track leads out across the fields. In the third field, continue

The view from Wintour's Leap

beyond the end of the hedge to the far side. At the corner, slip through a gap on the left and straight away turn right through a kissing-gate. Follow the field edge toward houses, a path between them leading out to the road **E**.

Turn right, almost immediately passing the superb viewpoint of Wintour's Leap on the left. It takes its name from Sir John Wintour, a man of local import during the 17th century, who leased extensive mining and timber rights in the Forest of Dean from the crown to supply his flourishing iron business. During the Civil War he sided with the Royalists and on one occasion, is supposed to have escaped the pursuit of Parliamentarian forces by leaping on horseback from the top of the cliff to be subsequently picked up from the river by a boat. History records his survival for he was later captured and spent time in the Tower of London, eventually returning to the forest to resume his iron making. His miraculous escape is more likely the result of him knowing a precarious path down the cliff, but that would not make for nearly so good a tale.

Be careful beside the road, for this stretch has no accompanying footway or verge. Past Netherhope Lane, walk for some 30 yds beyond a bus shelter to leave over a stile on the right from which Offa's Dyke Path is signed **F**. Head away at the edge of a meadow to a kissing-gate and continue through a dark wood. Ignore a stile near the corner and curve left with the boundary. Later coming out of the wood, walk on at the perimeter of a field, and then at the far side, pass through three kissing-gates in quick succession to regain the main road.

Carry on up the hill for almost ½ mile before quitting the road over a stile, this time on the left **G**. A contained path delves through trees to meet Offa's Dyke. It was constructed by the Mercian king in the 8th century as the boundary between his kingdom and Wales and ran for 150 miles from the River Severn to the mouth of the River Dee. The path follows it at the edge of an almost precipitous drop into the river valley. Eventually the way swings right and then left, losing height to meet a track **H**. Abandon Offa's Dyke Path and take the track right, back out to the road.

Go left to a fork and branch off left along Miss Grace's Lane **J**. Miss Grace lived in Chase House during the early part of the last century and the lane now gives its name to a cave system opened at the end of the 20th century. With some 2¾ miles of surveyed tunnels and passageways it is the third largest known in the area, and implies a potential for further significant discoveries in the Forest of Dean's limestone.

After ½ mile at the end of the tarmac, turn off along a barriered path on the right onto the heath **K**. At a junction beside a triangulation pillar, go right and then bear left to return to the car park. Felling has restored the open aspect of the heath that existed before its afforestation in 1962. This has encouraged a greater variety of wildlife to the area, in particular attracting stonechat, linnet and nightjar as well as lizards and snakes. ●

Monmouth and the Kymin

		GPS waypoints	
Start	Monmouth		
Distance	7 miles (11.3km)	✐	SO 504 125
Height gain	835 feet (255m)	**Ⓐ**	SO 512 127
		Ⓑ	SO 535 101
Approximate time	3½ hours	**Ⓒ**	SO 529 115
Parking	Monmouth	**Ⓓ**	SO 527 125
Route terrain	Riverside and field paths, track and quiet lane	**Ⓔ**	SO 515 126
Ordnance Survey maps	Landranger 162 (Gloucester & Forest of Dean), Explorer OL14 (Wye Valley & Forest of Dean)		

Beginning in the ancient border town of Monmouth, the walk follows the Wye past its confluence with the River Monnow to the village of Redbrook. It then seeks the high ground to return along a section of the Offa's Dyke National Trail past two striking monuments. One commemorates the great naval admirals of the late 18th century while the other reflects the elegant dining and social habits of the Monmouth gentry and offers a grand panorama across the surrounding countryside.

Henry V was born in the gatehouse of Monmouth's castle, originally built by William Fitz-Osbern shortly after the Normans invaded England. Of the castle almost nothing remains, but there is a splendid 13th-century fortified bridge over the River Monnow, remarkably preserved and unique in the country. The town's other famous son was Charles Rolls, co-founder of the Rolls-Royce company. His partnership with Royce began in 1904, Royce providing the technical skill and Rolls providing finance for the company and selling the cars. But Rolls was a born adventurer; a keen balloonist, pioneer motorist and aviator. He was a founder member of the Royal Aero Club and amongst his flying achievements was the first non-stop double crossing of the English Channel in 1910. However, barely a month after his record-breaking flight,

he was killed when his plane broke up during a flying display at Bournemouth. There is an interesting exhibition describing his achievements at the Monmouth Museum.

✐ Start from the 13th-century fortified bridge across the River Monnow at the bottom end of the town, walking straight up the broad high street. Beyond the Shire Hall, bear right along the pedestrianised Church Street, at the end of which, by the parish church, turn right along St Mary's Street. At the bottom, go left and right towards the main road, using the subway on the left to reach the bridge over the River Wye. On the far bank, walk on a few yards before turning off right along a drive to Monmouth School Sports Ground **Ⓐ**.

Through the car park, bear right on a footpath that skirts the perimeter of the playing field, later coming beside the river to pass beneath a steel girder bridge erected in 1874 that took the railway from Monmouth to Ross-on-Wye. A little farther on, only the massive stone arches of the approach viaduct remain of an earlier bridge that took the Wye Valley line south to Chepstow. The central girder span was dismantled after the railway finally closed in 1964.

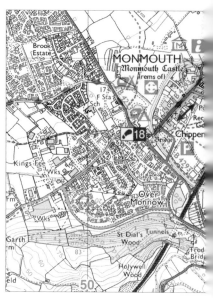

The path continues by the river, alternating between woodland and pasture before eventually turning you onto the main road at the edge of Redbrook. Follow the road towards the village and take the first turning on the left **B**. Walk up the hill for almost ¼ mile before branching off left at a National Trail waypost. A rough tarmac lane continues up the hill, bending left and reaching Duffield's Farm. Degrading to a track the way progresses steadily up a long tongue of hill for a further ½ mile, ultimately ending at stables, Cockshoot Ash Barn. Walk past the building on a grass path and slip through a kissing-gate **C** a few yards farther on to continue at the edge of a field.

Beyond a gate, keep going across the

The Round House on the Kymin

slope of the field, passing through another couple of gates to follow an enclosed path above the edge of a wood. The path subsequently rises at the edge of a meadow before reaching another contained path through a belt of thick wood. Emerge to cross the National Trust car park at the Kymin, from which a path leads onward past the Naval Temple to the Round House.

The Round House was erected in 1794 by members of the local gentry as a venue for their weekly gatherings, where they would dine well, enjoying their mutual company. There was a kitchen to prepare the food, served in the circular dining room, and on fine days, telescopes were erected in the room. In 1800, the Kymin Club, as it was known, commissioned the Naval Temple to commemorate the second anniversary

of the British victory over the French in the Battle of the Nile. It incorporates 16 plaques, one each for the top Admirals of the day.

After admiring the view, take a gravel path beyond the Round House into trees, where to the left, an intermittently stepped path descends steeply through Beaulieu Wood **D**. Coming out onto a lane, follow it downhill around a bend and then, in front of a cottage, leave through a kissing-gate on the right. A path slopes diagonally down across Beaulieu Meadows to a kissing-gate at the top of Garth Wood.

Offa's Dyke Path is signed to the left. Emerging onto the bend of a lane, walk down to a second bend and there carry on ahead along a drive. Where that in turn bends, keep ahead on a waymarked path into more trees. It ultimately descends to the main road **E**, which you should follow left, swinging around to the Wye Bridge and back into Monmouth.

Hay-on-Wye, Mouse Castle Wood and Cusop (vertical side title)

Hay-on-Wye, Mouse Castle Wood and Cusop

Start	Hardwicke
Distance	7¾ miles (12.5km)
Height gain	785 feet (240m)
Approximate time	3½ hours
Parking	Small car park on B4348 by junction with B4352
Route terrain	Field paths and some lanes
Ordnance Survey maps	Landranger 161 (The Black Mountains), Explorer OL13 (Brecon Beacons National Park - Eastern area)

GPS waypoints

✍	SO 263 439
Ⓐ	SO 265 432
Ⓑ	SO 261 423
Ⓒ	SO 249 424
Ⓓ	SO 243 421
Ⓔ	SO 239 414
Ⓕ	SO 235 417
Ⓖ	SO 229 422
Ⓗ	SO 234 426
Ⓙ	SO 244 439
Ⓚ	SO 256 450

Renowned for its antiquarian bookshops and festivals, picturesque Hay-on-Wye makes a grand focal point for this countryside ramble. Along the way is Mouse Castle, a Norman motte-and-bailey perched on the edge of the rising hills overlooking the old market town.

✍ Walk from the car park to the junction and go left towards Hay-on-Wye. After 100 yds cross a stile on the left and head out across the field to find another stile, just left of a gate in the far hedge. Maintain your direction across three more fields, dipping to pass through a gap breaking the trees Ⓐ. Carry on along the centre of a larger pasture, continuing beyond on a trod through the middle of a crop field.

Through a gap near the left end of the far hedge, cross a plank bridge. Cut the corner of the next field and dip across a wooded stream. Now continue along a flower-rich margin to emerge onto a lane by White House Farm Ⓑ.

Go left but leave after 20 yds, climbing to a stile in the right hedge. Walk beside a pair of barns and over a stile to carry on at the left boundary of a crop field. At the far corner, ignore the stile and instead swing right. Keep going at the edge of successive fields.

In the fourth field, the hedge now on your right, walk on to a gate and join a field track through a second gate. Abandon the track at that point, going left beside the hedge. Just before the corner, go left through a field gate and climb away past Ty-bordy, the cottage on the other

SCALE 1:27777 or 2¼ INCHES to 1 MILE 3.6CM to 1KM

side of the hedge. Emerge at the corner onto the bend of a gravel track **C**.

A narrow grass track opposite descends to a gate into Mouse Castle Wood. Where the path then splits, that to the right climbs to a castle tump. Mouse Castle is an early Norman motte-and-bailey and, although now much overgrown, would have held a commanding view across the Wye Valley. The ongoing route, however, takes the left branch, descending between the trees. Bear left again at the next fork, dropping steeply to a stile at the bottom of the wood. Carry on ahead across sloping fields to emerge onto a lane opposite Llydyadyway **D**.

Go left for almost 400 yds, looking for a stile on the right. Cross to a kissing-gate and keep going, joining a hedge on the left. Passing through the corner into a buttercup meadow, strike a shallow diagonal to find a kissing-

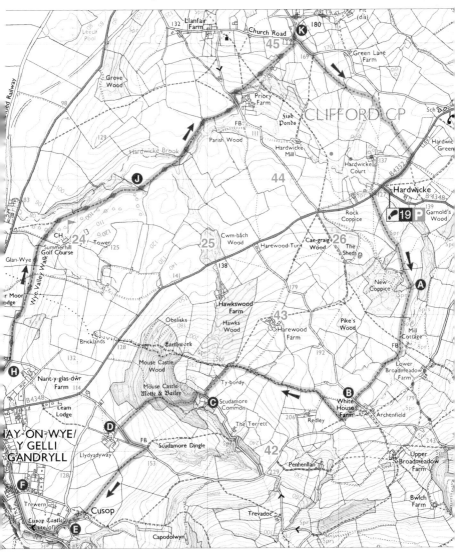

gate at the far side, which leads into St Mary's churchyard at Cusop. Walk through and leave by the lychgate at a junction of lanes **E**. Take the one opposite, which passes the site of Cusop Castle and wind pleasantly downhill to join the main lane.

Follow it right, but just after passing a junction turn in left beside a house, Rosedale **F**, and then swing right along a tarmac path signed to the footbridge. Cross Dulas Brook and climb away between a couple of cottages, the ongoing path cutting the corner of a field to reach a gate. Walk away at the edge of a couple of fields, leaving by a gate at the far-right corner. A track leads up to the main road near the entrance of Hay-on-Wye's main car park **G**.

Cross to the street opposite and walk into the old town. At a junction beside **Kilverts Hotel**, the market hall and square in front of the castle lie to the left and scattered along the narrow streets you will find all the bookshops. Otherwise, the ongoing route lies to the right along Bear Street.

After being battered alternately by both English and Welsh, Hay-on-Wye's castle was largely demolished to make way for a mansion, but its remaining keep is said to be the oldest in Wales. The nearby buttermarket was erected in 1830 on the site of an earlier market square and now renovated serves as the focus of the town's Thursday Market.

Emerging onto another main street go right and then left before the **Old Black Lion**. Where the ginnel forks, bear right, descending steeply past cottages to a bridge across Dulas Brook. On the far bank, climb left into a large pasture and strike north east across it to find a stile at the far side. Drop left to a slab bridge in a wooded gully and climbing out, continue at the edge of a smaller field to emerge onto a lane **H**.

Go forward to the next bend, leaving there along a short track and through a gate into the corner of a field. Head away following Wye Valley Walk symbols, roughly maintaining your direction from field to field and eventually reaching the edge of a golf course. With an eye open for play, cross the fairway to a drive and keep going, watching for wayposts that curve you right along the far edge of the course beside a belt of trees. Higher up, just past the tee for the 14th hole, watch for a waypost swinging you right along a strip of rough. Farther on, another marker directs you left across the fairway to a stile out of the course **J**.

Strike out across a rough pasture, joining the right hedge. At the far corner, cross a bridge beside a ford over Hardwicke Brook and follow a field track that shortly ends at a lane opposite Priory Farm.

Go left, taking the first track off on the right over a cattle-grid towards Priory House. Keep left where it forks, continuing beyond its end to a stile at the top of the field. Carry on to the upper right corner of the next field from which a hedged path leads to a junction of lanes **K**.

Go right towards Dorestone and Bredwardine, leaving after 350 yds at a bend over a stile beside a double gate on the right. Take the path signed half left. Cross to a stile partway along the boundary and maintain the same direction down to another stile in the left corner. Head out across the next field to a gate and keep going across the field beyond to an internal corner by an oak. Follow the ongoing boundary into the corner and keep going straight across two final fields onto the B4352. Turn right and then at a junction, go left back to the car park at Hardwicke. ●

Goodrich Castle

		GPS waypoints
Start	Goodrich	
Distance	8¼ miles (13.3km)	✎ SO 575 195
Height gain	310 feet (95m)	Ⓐ SO 574 193
		Ⓑ SO 580 192
Approximate time	3½ hours	Ⓒ SO 587 177
Parking	Goodrich Castle car park (check noticeboard for closing times)	Ⓓ SO 569 170
		Ⓔ SO 574 184
Route terrain	Field paths, tracks and quiet lane	
Ordnance Survey maps	Landranger 162 (Gloucester & Forest of Dean), Explorer OL14 (Wye Valley & Forest of Dean)	

Almost throughout its length, the Wye writhes and squirms between the low hills of the southern Welsh borderlands, at times almost meeting itself. Downstream of Goodrich Castle is no exception as the river enters a narrowing gorge. The walk follows its splendid course down to the foot of the famous Symonds Yat Rock before climbing back over the 'isthmus'.

Goodrich Castle is remarkably intact; massively thick walls connect great, buttressed towers set at the cardinal points and enclose a courtyard surrounded by domestic and ceremonial quarters and the original keep. It lies just a short walk from the car park, where the visitor centre incorporates a **café**.

Godric Mappeston held the manor in the 11th century, fortifying this rocky spur above the river. But these were troubled times and under King Stephen, it passed to the Earls of Pembroke. Richard de Clare the second earl improved it with a keep, bringing stone along the river from the Forest of Dean. Outer walls were added by William Marshal in the 13th century. However, the whole was rebuilt when the earldom and castle passed to William de Valance, half-brother to Henry III. He constructed the massive defensive towers and imposing barbican, creating a deep moat and making the place well-

nigh impregnable. Indeed, it was not until the Civil War of 1642 that the technology of belligerence seriously threatened its defences. Although initially held for the Parliamentarians, the position was vulnerable within the predominantly Royalist Welsh Marches and they made a tactical withdrawal. But in 1646 they were back and laid siege to the fortress. The King's men held out for over four months before the Parliamentarians rolled up 'Roaring Meg', the ultimate weapon of its day, which breached the walls with its 200 pound shot.

From the car park, go back down the castle drive to a junction in the village Ⓐ and turn left, following the lane over a bridge. Immediately mount a stile on the left and descend to the main road. Walk away from the bridge. Just before Kerne Bridge, cross a stile on the right Ⓑ, drop to a riverside path and head downstream.

Passing through both field and woodland, the path imparts its greatest delight in spring and early summer, when a succession of wildflower meadows come into bloom. At first the path follows a section of the former Ross and Monmouth Railway, but after ¾ mile, the line took a 600-yard

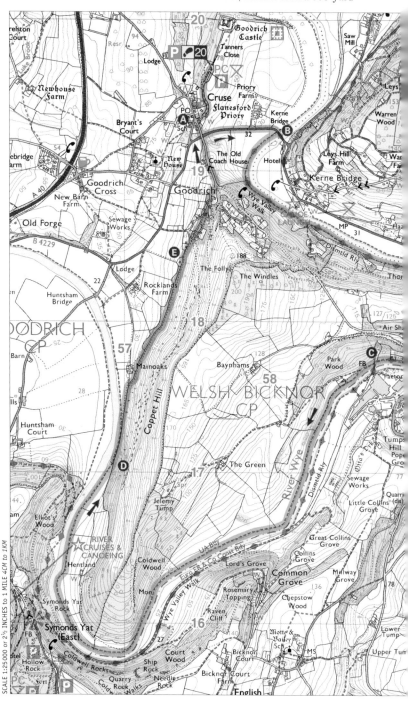

shortcut beneath the hill to Welsh Bicknor, shortening a 2½-mile loop of the river. The path remains with the river, which describes a sweeping turn in front of Lower Lydbrook on its way to Welsh Bicknor.

Courtfield, which overlooks the river from the high hill enclosed within the bend is the seat of the manor and is reputedly where Henry V was nursed during infancy. St Margaret's, the parish church, is situated by the river and was built in 1858 at the expense of the then rector to replace an earlier church. The adjacent Youth Hostel was the former Rectory and is of a later date than the church.

The Wye

Leaving the meadows behind, the path carries on through woodland, in a little while reaching a skeletal railway bridge **C**. It took the line from the southern portal of the tunnel across the river. There, an abandoned factory complex started life as a wireworks, which produced cables for field telephones during the First World War. The riverside path continues, shortly following the edge of a succession of pastures. Much later, passing into more woodland, look out for a railinged monument to the memory of John Warre who, at the age of 16, drowned here in front of his distraught and helpless parents.

The path breaks into the open as it runs below Coldwell Rocks and Symonds Yat, eventually leaving the cliffs behind to re-enter trees at the foot of Coppet Hill **D**. Follow the track through the wood and on towards Mainoaks Farm. Approaching the farm entrance, leave over a stile on the right into the Coppet Hill Common Nature Reserve.

The path rakes across the slope, in time emerging from the trees above Rockland Cottage **E**. Walk on to join a track, passing more cottages and finally meeting a narrow lane. Follow the lane left, keeping left at a fork. Stride out down the hill, re-crossing the bridge over the main road and retracing your steps back to the castle car park. ●

Fownhope, Brockhampton and Capler Camp

		GPS waypoints
Start	Fownhope	🥾 SO 578 340
Distance	7½ miles (12.1km)). Shorter version 4½ miles (7.2km)	**Ⓐ** SO 587 328 **Ⓑ** SO 584 312
Height gain	1,115 feet (340m). Shorter version 770 feet (235m)	**Ⓒ** SO 588 316 **Ⓓ** SO 596 315
Approximate time	4 hours (2½ hours for shorter version)	**Ⓔ** SO 594 321 **Ⓕ** SO 590 324
Parking	By recreation ground off Capler Lane	**Ⓖ** SO 598 333 **Ⓗ** SO 589 346
Route terrain	Quiet lanes, tracks and field paths	
Ordnance Survey maps	Landranger 149 (Hereford & Leominster), Explorer 189 (Hereford & Ross-on-Wye)	

The high ground overlooking the Wye Valley offered a perfect vantage for the early peoples who settled here and several Iron Age settlements have been identified along its course. One of the most imposing is Capler Camp, reached here from the tiny village of Fownhope.

🥾 Walk from the car park to Capler Lane and go right, following it out of the village over hill and dale for a mile. As the lane eventually begins to climb along the wooded flanks of Capler Hill, watch for a waymarked track branching down to the right **Ⓐ**.

The shorter walk remains with the lane, rising to rejoin the long route at a viewpoint at the top of the hill **Ⓕ**. The main route, however, takes the falling track. Ignore a footpath signed off right a few yards along and remain with the track, which descends gently across the steep tree-clad slope to close with the River Wye. Progressing downstream around a sweeping bend, the view opens along the valley meadows, where the tall spire of Ballingham church can be seen on the opposite bank.

When the track forks after a mile, bear left, climbing steeply to a lane beside Brinkley Hill picnic area **Ⓑ**. Go left through the hamlet for a little over ¼ mile to find a track leaving sharply right beside a cottage, signed as the Wye Valley Walk **Ⓒ**. Follow a grass track away between the fields, turning left when you reach a junction. Now enclosed between tall hedges, it ultimately leads to another lane.

Turn right, but after some 250 yds, take a roughly metalled track on the left. Follow it down into a dip, departing there over a stile beside a gate on the left **Ⓓ**. Walk away along a developing trod at the base of a shallow valley. The hamlet's original church stood on the hill above to the right near Brockhampton Court, but was replaced

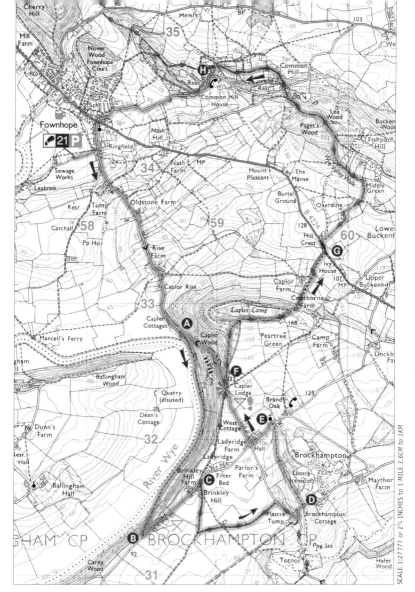

SCALE 1:27 777 or 2¼ INCHES to 1 MILE 3.6CM to 1KM

with a new church, which soon comes into view at the head of the valley.

One of the few thatched churches in the country, it was only completed in 1902 and is a charming example of Arts and Crafts design. Deeply splayed windows admit an intimate light to the body of the building, which is decorated with carved panels of flowers on the choir stalls and tapestries designed by Burne-Jones and made in William Morris's workshops. Those interested in this genre of architecture might also visit nearby Kempley, whose 'new' church dedicated to St Edward the Confessor was finished the following year.

Coming out onto a lane **E**, follow it left as far as a crossroads, there turning right towards Fownhope and Hereford. It climbs to a viewpoint overlooking the river from the crest of the hill. Meeting the shorter version of the walk just beyond a lodge **F**, branch off right with the Wye Valley Walk along a track. Emerging at a junction in a clearing, bear right with the waymarked path, cutting through a conifer plantation to meet another track below the double embankments of Capler Camp. Go right and then keep ahead as the track curves left to broach the defences, following a path to a small gate and stile.

Encircling the summit of the hill in an elongated oval are impressive earthworks, which are thought to have been dug around 500BC. Although they suggest a defensive purpose, archaeological excavation in 1924 found no evidence of internal structures and concluded that the site may never have been occupied. However, a recent geophysical survey revealed traces of a round-house and storage pit, renewing speculation as to what the site might have been used for; perhaps a refuge, tribal village or seasonal livestock enclosure.

Entering open grazing, the path continues between the ramparts, shortly passing beside a disused barn. As a track then develops, swing left at a waymark tacked to a tree, heading down to a stile. A stepped path drops steeply through trees, exiting the bottom of the wood over a stile into the corner of a field. Carry on at the left edge of a couple of fields, finally mounting a stile hidden in the left corner to enter a yard at Caplor Farm. Go left to a track and there turn right, following it out to a lane **G**.

Walk up the hill, leaving after 50 yds along a broad track on the right. After a few yards, cross a stile on the right and bear left downfield, looking for a stile in the high hedge partway along. Continue descending the hill with the hedge now on your right and swing within the bottom corner to a gate gap. Pass through into the adjacent field and climb away by the left hedge. Ignore the first stile and carry on to find another in the top corner. Over that, bear left by the fence to yet another stile beneath a sprawling oak in the corner. The way then progresses along the upper edge of a succession of narrow meadows into Paget's Wood.

Take the path into the trees past the information board. Ignore a path off left and carry on to a junction a little farther on. Bear left on a broad path past a blue waypost (not the grass path more immediately left beside the fence). Descend gently through the trees, leaving over a stile to walk along a track. As the way broadens to a field, keep right beside a fence at the edge of a wood, passing through a couple of gates to emerge on a narrow lane in front of a cottage.

Take the track opposite, keeping left at a fork behind the cottage. At the top, go through a small gate on the right, from which a path undulates along the crest of a wooded ridge. Breaking from the trees the way drops across a meadow to a gate at the bottom boundary of the nature reserve, from where a hedge-tunnelled path continues gently downhill to a junction. Take the second track on the left, which leads down to the bend of a lane **H**. Ahead it leads back to Fownhope. At a cross-roads beside the church, cross straight over and walk back to the car park.

Fownhope's church evolved from a small Norman chapel to become one of the largest village churches in the country. Inside you will find a 14th-century chest fashioned from the trunk of an oak tree and a beautifully carved sandstone tympanum, thought to have crowned a doorway of the early chapel. Beside the road at the front, the village stocks and whipping post are preserved. ●

Newnham and Soudley Ponds

		GPS waypoints
Start	Newnham	🚩 SO 693 120
Distance	8¼ miles (13.3km)	Ⓐ SO 691 118
Height gain	885 feet (270m)	Ⓑ SO 670 121
Approximate time	4 hours	Ⓒ SO 662 106
Parking	Newnham – long stay parking area	Ⓓ SO 665 103
		Ⓔ SO 669 088
Route terrain	Farm and woodland tracks, field paths	Ⓕ SO 686 098
		Ⓖ SO 688 113
Ordnance Survey maps	Landranger 162 (Gloucester & Forest of Dean), Explorer OL14 (Wye Valley & Forest of Dean)	

Beginning from the former Severn shipbuilding port of Newnham, the walk climbs to the eastern fringes of the Forest of Dean to follow the course of Soudley Brook, whose upper reaches have been dammed to create a sequence of ponds. The Dean Heritage Centre offers an opportunity for an interesting break in the ramble before returning across the fields and an attractive finish beside the River Severn.

The Romans exploited the Forest of Dean for its iron, bringing some of it to Newnham, where there was a low-water ford across the river. A Roman road came down the hill from Littledean, where the foundations of a Roman temple have been discovered. After the Norman invasion, the place grew to be a

Soudley Ponds

port of some importance, and Henry II sailed from here to invade Ireland with a flotilla of 400 ships. The town prospered as a middleman in transhipping cargoes up and down the Severn and providing a ferry across the river, its wealth reflected in the many fine buildings and an extensive wharf that date from its heyday during the 18th century. Boat building was important too, carried out at yards just downriver at Bullo Pill. Indeed as Newnham began to decline in the face of the railways, Bullo assumed the greater importance as a port because of its connections with the coalmines in the forest. However, the railways gradually obviated the need for coastal transport and Bullo's port finally closed in 1926.

Walk up the main street to the clock tower in the centre of the town **A**. Turn right along Station Road, continuing forward at a bend into Hyde Lane. After crossing the railway, keep ahead at another bend on a track towards cottages, but then almost immediately, bear off left before the first cottage, crossing its yard to a kissing-gate.

Strike a shallow diagonal up the field, maintaining the same line over the crest of the next field, joining the hedge to reach a gate. Rather than pass through onto the lane, follow a flagged path beside it. Over a footbridge, continue at the edge of the next field until you are then forced onto the lane. Walk uphill a short distance before turning in at the entrance drive to Staure. Leave the drive almost immediately

through a kissing-gate on the left and carry on at the field boundary as before. Entering the next field, bear across right to a kissing-gate in the middle of the rising hedge. Walk through to the field

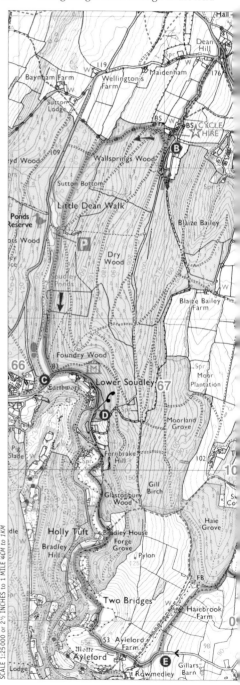

SCALE 1:25000 or 2½ INCHES to 1 MILE 4CM to 1KM

beyond and turn left, climbing behind Cockshoot Farm to a kissing-gate in the top corner of the field.

Cross to the gate opposite and turn right, descending beside the fence to another kissing-gate. Through that bear left, gaining height across the slope of the hill to the upper hedge. Back once more beside the lane, keep going towards houses at the top of the hill.

Emerging onto the lane at the edge of Littledean walk a few yards farther up the hill to a junction and double back left. Take the middle branch at a three-way split and follow the narrow lane towards the forest. After ¼ mile, bear right at a fork along a track running beside Blaize Bailey Cottage and past a barrier to a junction, a short distance into the forest **B**. The way lies sharp right but first bear left and then keep left at a fork to reach an arresting viewpoint. It looks out across the Severn Valley, where among the landmarks is the cathedral at Gloucester.

Return to the junction **B** and this time take the track leaving west of north. It quickly curves round to the left in a long and steady descent into the wooded valley. At the eventual bottom, walk out past a barrier and go left through a parking area, leaving along another barriered track at the far end. It falls beside the succession of Soudley Ponds, ultimately emerging onto a lane **C**.

The origin of the ponds has been the

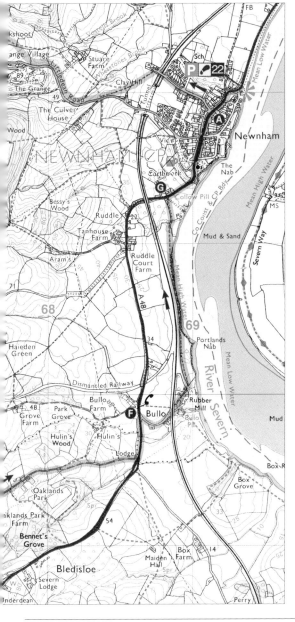

subject of considerable debate. At one time it was thought that they served iron furnaces lower down the valley and it was even suggested that they were medieval fishponds built by the monks of Flaxley Abbey, a Cistercian house some 3½ miles to the north east. However, although the lakes were in fact fishponds they were only created during the middle of the 19th century to improve the estate after William Crawshay, a Welsh ironmaster, bought it. Camp Mill, just down the lane, has its own pond and was built in the 18th century to grind corn. It now houses the Dean Heritage Centre whose interesting exhibitions describe the industrial and natural history of the forest. There are also gardens, a forester's cottage and craft workshops as well as a **café** serving local produce.

To the left, the lane leads past the Dean Heritage Centre continuing beyond to a junction beside a bridge **D**. Take the minor lane ahead, which leads past some cottages. After them, over to the left, is the western portal of the Haie Tunnel. Completed in 1810, the track was originally laid as a plateway using horse-drawn carriages to transport coal from Cinderford to a wharf at Bullo Pill. When built, at 1,083 yards long, Haie was the longest railway tunnel in the world. The following year, engineers tried to sink a tunnel beneath the River Severn, but water flooded in and the scheme was abandoned.

Continue with the ongoing track, keeping right through a gate on a waymarked bridleway where it shortly fragments. Bear left in front of the next gate to carry on through the pretty valley along a pleasant path. Reaching more cottages, the track re-asserts itself. Cross a bridge and then take the left fork. Eventually, beyond a row of stone cottages, swing left over a bridge to follow a narrow undulating lane. After ¼ mile, having crossed a brook climb to a right-hand bend and leave over a stile beside a gate on the left **E**.

Head across the slope of the meadow to a stile at the far side and keep going in the next meadow, picking up a hedge on your left. Passing through a hedge gap just right of the end corner, walk forward, putting a hedge on your left. Curve right above a bank of bracken and orchids to continue at the edge of a wood. After crossing a muddy ditch, immediately drop left to find a stile into the wood. Walk up to join a track and follow that to the right, winding over a low hill. Becoming a drive, it passes the estate offices and 18th-century mansion of Oaklands Park and a view of the Severn opens as it leads down to the main road.

Go left and then first right to Bullo Pill **F**. Some 50 yds after passing beneath a railway bridge turn left up a narrow path beside a stone wall, going right along a track at the top. As that then curves left, keep ahead on a contained path behind houses. At its end, walk forward across the head of another track to a kissing-gate from which a fenced path leads behind a stable block and on at the edge of paddocks.

Through another kissing-gate the path passes along a strip of woodland, emerging beyond that into an open meadow. Stride on above the river, towards the far end moving away to pass left of a sprawling oak. Pick up a hedged path, which shortly joins a farm track out to the main road **G**.

Go right towards Newnham, leaving on a bend to follow a path up into the churchyard of St Mary's. Emerging at the far side at the head of the main street, walk back down through the town to the start. ●

St Briavels and Hewelsfield

		GPS waypoints	
Start	St Briavels	✎	SO 558 046
Distance	8½ miles (13.7km)	Ⓐ	SO 552 043
Height gain	970 feet (295m)	Ⓑ	SO 539 051
Approximate time	4 hours	Ⓒ	SO 531 020
Parking	By St Briavels Castle	Ⓓ	SO 538 015
		Ⓔ	SO 544 015
Route terrain	Old tracks, field paths and	Ⓕ	SO 554 019
	quiet lanes	Ⓖ	SO 567 021
Ordnance Survey maps	Landranger 162 (Gloucester &	Ⓗ	SO 559 043
	Forest of Dean), Explorer OL14		
	(Wye Valley & Forest of Dean)		

Beginning from St Briavels on the Forest of Dean plateau, this walk drops to follow the Wye past Llandogo. After winding through a maze of old lanes the route regains the high ground up a wooded valley to reach the hamlet of Hewelsfield, picturesquely clustered around its sturdy church.

Although celebrating the memory of a Welsh saint, St Briavels came under English rule and its strategic location overlooking the river boundary between the two countries was fortified with an imposing castle.

✎ From the castle's 13th-century gatehouse, take the downhill lane towards Lower Meend, branching right at a fork. Merging with another lane, follow it around a hairpin bend past a junction but immediately leave sharp left for a path marked as a restricted byway. At its bottom, go right and then left down steps beside a house and carry on to emerge beside Tree Cottage Ⓐ.

Accompany the lane downhill, bearing off left to a stile just before its end at the gates of a water treatment plant. Cross a stream and turn right on a field track at the edge of the pasture. Keep going past Lindors Farm, eventually curving right and following the track out to the main road beside Bigsweir Bridge Ⓑ. The elegant arch

spans the River Wye at its tidal limit and was put up in 1827 to carry a turnpike between Chepstow and Monmouth. Spanning 160 feet, it is of cast iron and was made in Merthyr Tydfil.

Turn towards the bridge, but leave just before it left onto Offa's Dyke Path. Stay beside the bank across a couple of fields before joining a track near Bigsweir House where the river scurries noisily around a small island. Saunter to the right beneath umbrageous trees, keeping right when you later reach a fork to break out onto meadows that sweep beside the Wye past Llandogo. Farther on, as the river chatters over rapids, the path briefly re-enters woodland, but continues beyond along a narrow meadow at the far end of which is a small, stone boathouse Ⓒ.

There bear left, passing a solitary horse chestnut tree on your way to a kissing-gate. Cross the slope of a couple of small paddocks to carry on at the upper edge of a large pasture. After some 200 yds, slip through a gap stile to continue along the adjacent drive.

Coming to buildings fork left through a gate and follow a narrow lane up beside the cottage. Reaching a junction, go sharp left, but after 150 yds and just before Orchard Cottage, take a path on the right **D** signed as a restricted byway that climbs through the trees behind the house. Breaking cover, head up between fields to meet another narrow lane.

Turn right and keep right at the next junction. At a bend after a further 150 yds and immediately past Oakland House, leave right on another byway, once again on the Offa's Dyke Path. At the bottom go left and then right to continue with the byway. As the track subsequently swings through a gate, keep ahead across a stream and climb to a junction, there walking ahead out to another lane **E**. The village shop, which incorporates a **café**, is to be found just up the hill. The onward route, however, lies along the broad track directly opposite, parting company with the Offa's Dyke Path.

Descending gently into the valley, the track follows the stream, later taking you past a cottage. Where it subsequently swings left to a house, keep ahead on a rising tree-lined path, which before long leads out to a lane **F**.

Carry on up the hill, later joined by a couple of lanes from the left and eventually arriving at a crossroads with the B4228. Go straight over along Church Road to reach the tiny village of Hewelsfield, clustered around its ancient church.

Dedicated to St Mary Magdalene, the foundation is Saxon, from which time there is a 1,300 year-old yew still standing in the graveyard. It was rebuilt during the early Norman period and the tower contains the oldest ringable

church bell in the forest, while over the porch is a tiny hermit's cell.

Bear left with the lane around the churchyard, turning left at a junction **G** and heading down to a sharp bend. Go left again along a short grass track behind a converted barn, which continues beyond as an old, forgotten lane. Mounting a stone stile at its end, amble on at the edge of a field, where views open across the rolling countryside and behind you to the Severn Valley. Over a stile just right of

SCALE 1:27777 or 2¼ INCHES to 1 MILE 3.6CM to 1KM

the next corner, the path resumes within a narrow strip of woodland. At the end, walk out to a metalled farm track by Aylesmore Court.

Turn right and immediately left on a track, rising through trees to a gate and stile. Go through to a second gate, but ignore that in preference to a stile in the hedge a couple of yards to its left. Head away with the hedge on your right, passing through a succession of large fields. Eventually, partway along the fifth field as you approach St Briavels, watch for a stile and slip through the hedge to continue along a rough track on its other side.

Reaching the main road **H**, cross to the truncated street opposite and walk down to a junction by the **Crown Inn**. Bear right down Pystol Lane to a cross-roads and keep ahead to walk around the castle walls back to the start. ●

Speech House, Cannop Ponds and Edge End

		GPS waypoints	
Start	Speech House picnic site		SO 623 124
Distance	8½ miles (13.7km)	**A**	SO 619 122
Height gain	1,015 feet (310m)	**B**	SO 627 108
Approximate time	4 hours	**C**	SO 619 096
Parking	Car park at start	**D**	SO 608 100
Route terrain	Woodland tracks and paths	**E**	SO 609 107
Ordnance Survey maps	Landranger 162 (Gloucester & Forest of Dean), Explorer OL14 (Wye Valley & Forest of Dean)	**F**	SO 592 113
		G	SO 596 134
		H	SO 610 128

The 17th-century Speech House is at the heart of the royal forest and is a good base from which to explore. Features passed on this ramble include an arboretum, forest lakes and the line of a former railway, one of several that served the many mines and quarries that were once worked in the area.

Built in 1676 under Charles II, whose arms appear inside above the door to the verderers' court, Speech House was part of the King's grand plan to reorganise the forest. It was one of six built at the time, each housing a verderer to control a section of woodland known as a walk. This was originally called King's Lodge and served both as a hunting lodge and centre from which the forest laws were administered – the Court of Speech from which the building's present name derives. Dean was a royal forest even before the arrival of the Normans, King Canute appointing verderers to oversee the workings of the forest, protect its timber and the animals that roamed wild within its bounds. Strict laws governed what could and could not be done, particularly with regard to the felling of trees, grazing animals and of course hunting game. Poaching deer

was a capital offence and a gibbet once stood on the green outside Speech House for the execution of convicted felons. The verderers still meet in the Speech House courtroom every 40 days, and while nobody has been hanged for some considerable time (although apparently the power to impose the sentence still exists, the gibbet has been lost), the court continues to oversee many aspects of forest life.

Begin along a track signed to Beechenhurst Lodge, which leaves the car park behind an information board. At a junction, bear left remaining parallel with the road to reach a gate **A**. Instead of passing through, turn left up to Speech House. Cross to follow the lane opposite towards Park End, Yorkley and Blakeney, beside which stand a row of commemorative oaks. After 300 yds, bear off left along a track towards the Cyril Hart Arboretum.

Speech House Lake

The Arboretum was established 100 years ago and contains over 400 specimen trees. It was named for Cyril Hart OBE in 1999. Throughout his life he has been passionate about the forest and just about every aspect of its history and was elected a Verderer in 1952.

Beyond the car park and picnic area, pass through a gate and carry on along a broad, straight avenue. Walk ahead at a crossroads, but then later, turn off right to Speech House Lake. Keep left along its eastern shore, curving onto the dam at the far end. After passing above an outflow stream, turn left on a narrow path that drops beside it.

Reaching a junction at Reform Bridge **B**, go sharp right. Climb gently to another junction with Trafalgar Avenue, which was planted in 2005 with 200 oak trees to commemorate the 200th anniversary of the Battle of Trafalgar. Bear left, eventually meeting a lane.

Cross to the continuing track opposite and keep ahead at a diagonal crossing, a little farther along. The trail heads downhill at the edge of a recently felled area, opening the hillside to the left. Carry on to a junction at the bottom, known as the Three Brothers **C**. Under the shade of the oak trees that once grew here, colliers from the local mines would gather for Sunday morning union meetings. Sadly, only one of the oaks still stands.

Remain with the main track as it swings right around the surviving tree and stride on steadily downwards for a good ½ mile to a junction at Cannop Wharf **D**. Go left and then immediately right along a path leading to a bridge spanning the outflow of Cannop Ponds. However, rather than cross the bridge, veer right again on a path beside the lake.

At the head, where the lake disappears into reeds and marsh, continue with the waymarked path, which winds out to a picnic area by a car park. Keep left around the edge of the grass to a bridge over a stream **E** and carry on along the dam holding back the upper lake to reach the main road.

Cross to the track opposite, but where that then swings into a car park, bear left past a barrier to follow a gently ascending path between saplings. Disregard a green track and carry on through mature timber, climbing to a forest trail. Walk ahead over that, still heading upwards to reach a rough track. Ignore that too and keep going, later curving left beside a fence above a quarry.

Stay forward as a track rises from the right and then bear right along another rough track to run above the recently felled slopes of Howlers Slade. Meeting a foresters' road at the far end of the felled area, cross to the narrow path opposite, which leads into mature trees. At a waymarked fork, branch right and then a few yards farther on at a crosspath, go right, again following waymarks to come out onto the main road just outside Broadwell **F**.

Take the track opposite, keeping left at a fork to continue along a tarmac drive. Some 50 yds around a bend, look for a waypost indicating a path off left into the trees. Indistinct yellow arrows on trees nudge you right to a crossing of paths. Go ahead through scrub around the fenced perimeter of an open meadow, formerly a camping ground.

Ignore two crossing paths but then bear right to pick up a line of power cable posts. In a little while meeting a broad forest road, go left curving around the cleared head of Wimberry Slade. After some ½ mile, just where the trail crests, leave left at a waypost. Initially a narrow path, the way shortly becomes more defined through the trees and eventually leads to a six-way crossing. Take the middle path of the three ahead, which before long meets the main road at a barrier **G**.

Turn right away from the road, remaining with the main track as it winds easily downhill. Some 250 yds after a right-hand bend, watch for a waypost indicating a path to the left. Climb beside an area of sweet chestnut trees, dropping beyond the rise to another forest road. The waymarked path continues diagonally opposite, now losing height determinedly to meet a crossing path. Go straight over on an

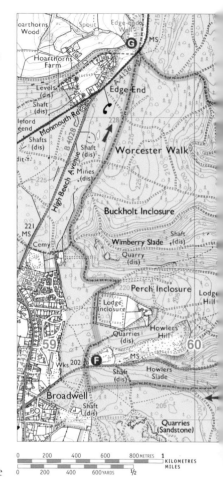

undulating grass path, keeping right at a fork and soon reaching another foresters' road. Again cross diagonally to the trail opposite, following that out to a road **H**.

Cross to a footpath that heads to a footbridge, climbing beyond to a cycle path running along the embankment of a former railway. Through a gate opposite, drop off the embankment and follow a path on up the hill. Towards the top, a path off right leads to a small abandoned quarry floor, which contains one of several sculptures dotted around this part of the forest. It is of interest for the pieces of fossilised wood embedded in the rock. Returning to the main path,

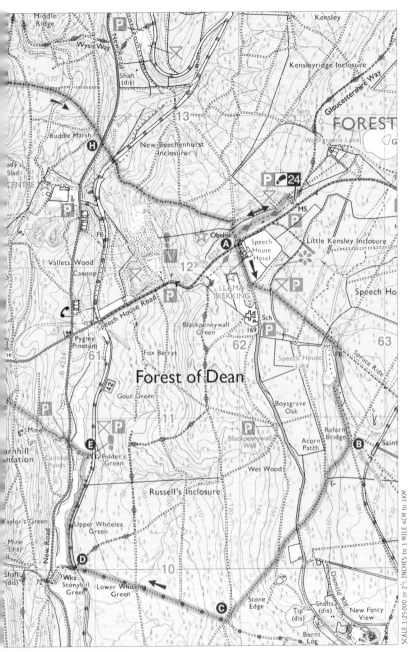

carry on to meet a forest road. Follow that ahead going over a crossing, the way now signed as the Beechenhurst and Sculpture trails. At the crest of the hill is another piece of forest art, a skeletal chair fashioned from hefty logs that looks out over the valley.

Keep going on the main trail, following yellow waymarks ahead when you reach a five-way junction. Later coming to a T-junction, go right, climbing beside a fence to a gate **A**. Pass through and retrace your outward route to the car park.

Dymock and Kempley Green

		GPS waypoints
Start	Queen's Wood, ¼ mile south of Kempley Green	🖉 SO 678 284
Distance	9½ miles (15.3km)	Ⓐ SO 677 288
Height gain	425 feet (130m)	Ⓑ SO 691 285
Approximate time	4½ hours	Ⓒ SO 700 311
Parking	Car park at start	Ⓓ SO 696 316
Route terrain	Field paths and tracks	Ⓔ SO 687 307
Ordnance Survey maps	Landranger 149 (Hereford & Leominster), Explorers 189 (Hereford & Ross-on-Wye), 190 (Malvern Hills & Bredon Hill) and OL14 (Wye Valley & Forest of Dean)	Ⓕ SO 682 306
		Ⓖ SO 673 315
		Ⓗ SO 668 310
		Ⓙ SO 662 296
		Ⓚ SO 665 292

March and April see the woods, meadows and orchards around Dymock and Kempley bathed in swathes of yellow as wild daffodils raise their trumpet heads to herald another spring. Such was their profusion that they inspired the 'Dymock Poets' and they still draw people to this corner of Gloucestershire every year. Passed along the way is Dymock parish church, where there is a year-round exhibition to the poets.

🖉 Follow the lane left out of the wood towards Kempley Green, but after ¼ mile just past a house Ⓐ, turn off right and immediately right again on a hedged grass path between it and its neighbour. Entering a field, walk away beside the hedge, continuing in the next field. Passing a large cattle shed, ignore a stile to the left and keep forward along the line set by a row of old apple trees. Beyond a kissing-gate, maintain your heading through the remnants of an orchard. Cross a stream beside an old pollarded willow and carry on to a kissing-gate into Dymock Wood.

Stay with the main gravelled path through the trees, ignoring a crossing path in the middle. Emerging onto a lane Ⓑ, go right over the motorway and at a T-junction turn left towards

Baldwins Oak. After ¼ mile, turn through a kissing-gate beside a gate on the left and wander down a narrow field, crossing back beneath the M50 at the far end. Coming out of the bridge, pass through a kissing-gate on the right and walk away below the motorway embankment. At the bottom corner of the second field, swing away from the motorway beside a tree-lined brook.

Leaving the field, cross a track to another kissing-gate opposite and keep with the ongoing hedge around to a metal gate. Through that join a track and follow it left. Where that swings into a farm, walk ahead along a field track, Boyce Court shortly coming into view. Reedy ponds to the right are remnants of the Hereford and Gloucester Canal, which operated for barely 40 years before it was closed in 1881.

Reaching a junction, turn right over a bridge and then drop left onto a path beside the former canal. After the canal disappears, cross a footbridge into the corner of a field. Carry on beside the boundary towards Dymock church, which can now be glimpsed ahead, half hidden by trees. At the far side of the second field, curve within the corner to find a kissing-gate. Cross a rough pasture and continue beside a meadow to emerge on the main road opposite the **Beauchamp Arms** **Ⓖ**. Cross the green facing you to the church.

Mentioned in the Domesday Book, St Mary's dates back to at least 1085, but is probably far older and there is speculation that it could have evolved from a Saxon monastery. Archaeological finds demonstrate that the area had been settled during the Roman period and by the Middle Ages, Dymock had developed as an important town. Dymock is associated with the King's Champion, an hereditary post dating back to the arrival of the Normans. Although now purely ceremonial, the King's Champion attended the coronation to take up the challenge of any who disputed the monarch's right to the crown. Created in 1066 it was held by the Marmions of Scrivelsby in Lincolnshire until the office was taken by Sir John Dymoke at the coronation of King Richard II after the male line died out, Sir John having married into the family.

In the church is a small exhibition to the 'Dymock Poets': Lascelles Abercrombie, Rupert Brooke, John Drinkwater, Robert Frost, Wilfrid Wilson Gibson and Edward Thomas. They came to live in the area in the years before the First World War and developed a more simplistic style, then considered 'modernist' that became known as Georgian Poetry.

Walk around the western end of the church below the tower, then leaving the path, bear right across the graveyard to a gate on the northern boundary. Head half-left across the field behind, taking a line past an indented corner and continuing beyond to a footbridge on the far boundary. However, ignore that and go left a short distance to a second bridge. Over that, cut left to a stile and exit onto a lane. Follow it right, meeting the main road at the far end **Ⓓ**.

The track opposite runs between the fields to Allum's Farm. After a little more than ¼ mile, abandon the track as it bends away from the hedge, staying beside the boundary. As you then pass the buildings, swing left to the back corner of a barn and keep going, straightening the jagged edge of the field behind the farm and its outbuildings to a gate at the far side. Bearing right, walk away through an orchard, picking up the hedge to the left. Through a kissing-gate in the corner, carry on at the edge of the next field to exit by a gate onto a lane **Ⓔ**.

Follow the lane right to meet a belt of woodland, leaving immediately before it over a stile on the right **Ⓕ**. Walk away beside Allums Grove, crossing into a second meadow. Now strike a diagonal to find a footbridge over a stream near the far right corner. Walk on to cross a second bridge and pass through a kissing-gate into the wood. The path is to the right, turning within the corner and rising to a kissing-gate. Briefly slip into the adjacent field, following the boundary to the corner where a kissing-gate takes you back into Allums Grove. Identified by occasional wayposts, a clear path weaves through the conifers, later broadening and leading to a crossing. Keep ahead, shortly exiting the wood into the corner of a field.

Heading out, skirt left of a clump of trees to find a footbridge in the corner beyond. Over that, walk away by the left hedge, swinging half-left at its end across the internal corner to a kissing-gate in the hedge. Follow the field edge to the right, curving within the corner to a footbridge hidden a short way along the high hedge. Over that, bear half-left across the corner to a hedge stile and maintain the same heading across a final field. Emerge onto a lane **G** and go left, in a little while reaching St Mary's Church.

It is presumed that St Mary's was founded by Hugh de Lacy, one of William's knights during the conquest of England, and who came into the manor after the death of his father and the rebellion of his elder brother against William. Hugh also founded the priory at Llanthony in the Vale of Ewyas, featured elsewhere in this collection of walks.

The simple, early chapel is famed for its wonderful set of medieval frescos, the oldest, those in the chancel, being completed at the time of the church's construction around 1120. As with many medieval stained glass windows, they served as visual aids to help the priest expand upon his Latin texts to a largely illiterate congregation. The roof of the chancel shows Christ in Majesty attended by four standing seraphim and four figures symbolising the evangelists, an angel for Matthew, a lion for Mark, a winged ox for Luke and an eagle for John. Near the arch are St Peter with his keys and Mary holding a church. On the side walls are the apostles and beyond the windows are two other figures carrying swords, assumed to be Hugh and his father Walter. Still vivid is a 15th-century wheel showing the ten ages of man and from a later age, remnants of texts

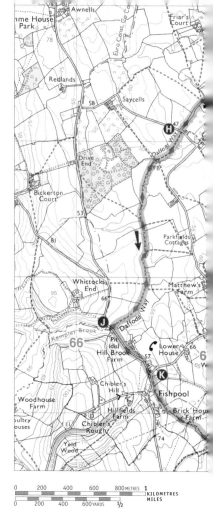

including the Lord's Prayer. The pictures were whitewashed over in the middle of the 16th century and only rediscovered in 1872 by the Reverend Arthur Drummond the then vicar.

Continue along the lane to a T-junction **H**, marked by a commemorative oak to the 7th Earl of Beauchamp. Although the family seat was at Madresfield Court near Great Malvern, the family acquired the manor in 1866. Cross to a stile opposite and strike out past an electricity pole, keeping the same line to a gateway in the far bottom hedge. Walk on, moving left to follow the lazy meanderings of Kempley Brook hidden in the bordering

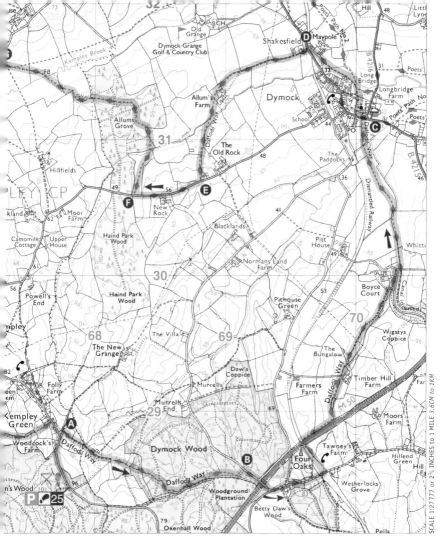

trees and bushes, which although largely unseen, is occasionally heard as it tumbles over periodic weirs. Carry on beside it from field to field, eventually emerging over a stile onto a narrow lane beside a bridge **J**.

Go left and later, at a junction **K**, turn right towards Upton Bishop, Linton and Ross. After some 50 yds, look for a stile hidden in the left hedge. Follow the hedge around right to another stile in the corner and carry on over more stiles from pasture to pasture. Keep straight ahead across a final field, making for a house in the middle distance. Over a footbridge at the far side of the field, a path leads behind stables to a wooden gate. Go through to meet a track by Moor House.

The onward way is over a stile beside a field gate facing you. Walk on at the right-hand edge of a paddock to a footbridge. Over that bear left cutting the corner of a meadow to another footbridge and wander on by the left boundary. Mounting a stile continue in the next field beside the hedge, following it around a curve. When it then shortly turns more sharply left, cut right across to a gate at the far corner. Emerging onto a lane, turn right and walk back the ½ mile to the car park. ●

Llanthony Priory and Hatterrall Hill

		GPS waypoints	
Start	Llanthony Priory	☑ SO 288 278	
Distance	8¾ miles (14.1km)	Ⓐ SO 291 259	
		Ⓑ SO 286 251	
Height gain	1,510 feet (460m)	Ⓒ SO 289 242	
Approximate time	4½ hours	Ⓓ SO 299 233	
Parking	Car park at start	Ⓔ SO 302 239	
Route terrain	Field paths, tracks and hill paths	Ⓕ SO 310 251	
Ordnance Survey maps	Landranger 161 (The Black Mountains), Explorer OL13 (Brecon Beacons National Park -Eastern area)	Ⓖ SO 312 254	
		Ⓗ SO 307 269	

The long ridges and deep valleys of the Black Mountains offer splendid walking, and this route from the evocative ruin of Llanthony Priory in the stunningly beautiful Vale of Ewyas reveals some of the finest scenery that this corner of Wales has to offer. After wandering through woodland and pasture it climbs to the hillside hamlet of Cwmyoy, whose tiny church has miraculously survived 700 years of subsidence. The onward ascent of Hatterrall Hill is rewarded by a satisfying ridge walk before descending to the priory.

Paths on the final section of the ascent of Hatterrall Hill are indistinct and the route is not recommended for inexperienced hill walkers in poor visibility.

Llanthony has been a religious site since the 6th century, when a small chapel dedicated to St David was established. Its name is an English corruption of Llandewi Nant Honddu, meaning 'the church of David on the River Honddu'. The best part of six centuries was to pass before the first priory was founded. By then the chapel was in ruins, but its remote beauty and spirituality moved William de Lacy, a Norman knight who chanced upon the spot when travelling with the Ernisius

priest to Queen Matilda, to build a new church, which he dedicated to St John the Baptist. Shortly afterwards, he founded a community for Augustinian canons, one of the first in Britain, emphasising a simple life in the belief that riches inhibited devotion to God. However, this was a wild and unruly place and the canons were soon forced to retreat to Gloucester in the face of local harassment. Things shortly settled and in 1186, Hugh de Lacy refounded the house, endowing sufficient funds to build a great priory church. Although fortunes fluctuated over the ensuing centuries, lying beside a pilgrim's route to St David's, it would have provided hospitality for those making the long and dangerous journey. However, being so remote, it remained vulnerable and by the time of the Dissolution it had already been taken over by its daughter house in Gloucester and only four canons remained.

By the beginning of the 19th century, the place was in ruins. The poet, Walter Savage Landor then bought it but despite sizeable investment to remodel it as an exemplar estate, non co-operation from neighbours and tenants eventually led him to abandon the place.

🖊 Leave the car park past the entrance to the priory and walk back to the main lane. Turn left but then immediately bear right to find a track leaving beside Mill Cottage signed to Bal Bach. After crossing a footbridge over the River Honddu, climb a stile directly in front and walk away at the field edge. After 50 yds, swing through a gap on the right, negotiate another stream and follow a diagonal rising trod across a couple of fields to reach a track. Cross to a stile opposite and maintain the same line up two more fields to emerge on another track.

The crooked church at Cwmyoy

Go left and at a split beyond a gate, branch right into the conifers of Llanthony Wood. Shortly passing a house, the track continues through the trees to merge with a second track. Entering more open ground, carry on through a gate, some 200 yds after which the track begins to curve right.

There **A**, fork off left along a narrow descending path, crossing a stream at the bottom. Through a gate, bear right at a junction above Upper Henllan Farm and continue on a track overshadowed by Tyle-ffardding Wood. Leaving the trees, pick your way across springs seeping from the rock to reach a broad forest track and follow that towards Noyaddllwyd Farm. However, some 70 yds along bear off left on a narrow path **B** hugging the wall behind the farmhouse to a stile. Advance along the upper edge of pasture below Coed Ty Canol. In time a stile takes the onward path into a conifer plantation. Shortly joining with a track from the right, continue down beyond the trees to pass a house. Over a stile, drop onto its track and keep with that out to the lane.

Go left but then after ¼ mile, just past a barn, take a track off on the right signed over the river to Cwmyoy **C**. Some 50 yds beyond a house, leave through a gap on the left and climb to a stile. Cross a track to a second stile opposite and walk away at the bottom of a pasture. Maintain the same line across the slope of the hill, the hedge subsequently appearing on your left. Where the boundary later curves away, keep ahead to leave at the far end of this final field over a stile beside a gate onto the bend of a track.

Follow it forward to emerge onto a lane and turn uphill to Cwmyoy. At a fork by a phone box bear left, passing the shell of a building where an apple press has been erected. Continue up into the hamlet, going left again **D** to the church.

St Michael's has been on the move since it was built in the 12th century, the ground on which it stands left unstable after the cliff above collapsed at the end of the last Ice Age. The nave and tower have slumped in opposite directions, twisting the building along its axis so much that the tower is said to tilt more than the Leaning Tower of Pisa.

Leave the churchyard through a gate in the north wall. Take the track left for a few yards and then turn right up a delightful hollow way signed to Graig. Through a gate at the top go right, the path running below cliffs and then climbing to a junction just past an abandoned cottage.

Walk ahead, shortly passing behind a large farmhouse. As the track then begins to curve down to the right **E**, branch off left up a bank and along a short grass track to a gate and stile. The ongoing path contours the hill beside the trees of an outgrown hedge. Keep going beyond the end of the boundary, bearing right at a fork, the path then gently falling to a gap in a wall. Cross a stream and swing right up to a gate and stile.

Instead of passing through, double back left along a grassy track that winds steeply up the hill, later settling beside a wall and leading to a gate from which there is a grand view down the valley. The way continues upwards, higher up veering right in a more direct assault of the slope. Subsequently curving left, the gradient eases as the path runs to a grassy clearing amid the bracken **F**. At this point, the best line of ascent is then to turn east, climbing past the mounds of old quarry workings and picking up a trod that leads to a wide footpath running north along the main ridge, Offa's Dyke Path. Follow that left, shortly reaching a junction of paths by a marker stone **G**, a little south east of the broad summit of Hatterrall Hill. Despite the flat top, there is a fine panorama to the south across the mouth of the River Severn to the distant Mendip Hills in Somerset.

Continue ahead along the main trail, dropping from the summit plateau onto the ridge that runs away to the north and which serves as the boundary between England and Wales. Superb views open on either side, the Vale of Ewyas and the central mass of the Black Mountains to the left, while beyond the Olchon Valley on the right are the distant Cotswold and Malvern Hills. After 1¼ miles, at another stone waypost **H**, leave the ridge for a narrower path bearing off left.

Joining a wall, the path heads steadily down across the slope of the hill. Keep left at a fork to cross a steep bank of bracken and gorse, the ruins of the priory coming into view ahead. Eventually the path levels to run beside a wire fence. Carry on for another ¼ mile until you reach a signpost.

Llanthony is signed left through a gate, down the edge of a field. Through another gate at the bottom, a path drops to the right through Wiral Wood. Emerging from the trees, continue downhill, heading towards the priory. Entering a meadow, skirt above the ruins and at the far side, turn left through a gate. Follow a track across a final field back to the start. ●

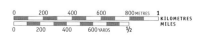

Symonds Yat and Highmeadow Woods

		GPS waypoints
Start	Symonds Yat Rock	SO 562 156
Distance	9¼ miles (14.9km)	**A** SO 561 157
Height gain	1,525 feet (465m)	**B** SO 549 143
Approximate time	4½ hours	**C** SO 544 140
Parking	Car park at start (Pay and Display)	**D** SO 546 126
Route terrain	Woodland tracks and paths	**E** SO 541 122
Ordnance Survey maps	Landranger 162 (Gloucester & Forest of Dean), Explorer OL14 (Wye Valley & Forest of Dean)	**F** SO 550 125
		G SO 559 120
		H SO 567 129

Symonds Yat Rock is one of the iconic features of the Forest of Dean, a striking viewpoint over a great crook of the River Wye and the starting point for this meandering circuit through a particularly beautiful corner of forest. Along the way it climbs steeply to two more stunning rocky eyries and incorporates a couple of other curiosities for good measure. Halfway round, Staunton offers refreshment and also has an interesting church.

From the car park toilets, take the signed Symonds Yat Trail, going left at a junction to the log cabin, where you can buy light refreshments. No one should miss out the dramatic viewpoint, which is reached along a wooden walkway spanning the road over to the right.

Retrace your steps towards the log cabin, but on leaving the walkway, bear right to find a stepped descending path. Approaching a road, swing left and continue downhill to another junction. Go left and immediately right down more steps before turning sharply left, the path now falling through the woods to emerge in front of the **Royal Lodge** at East Symonds Yat **A**.

Walk through the car park, looking up to see the Long Stone, a detached limestone pillar, which is a favourite with rock climbers. The ongoing path follows the course of an old railway beside the River Wye all the way to the Biblins suspension bridge. Apart from the hand-hauled rope ferries at Symonds Yat it is the only crossing point of the river between Goodrich and Monmouth. Originally put up in 1957 by the Forestry Commission, it was substantially rebuilt in 1997.

In a clearing just before the bridge **B**, go left on a strenuously climbing rough path. Watch for it veering right after some 250 yds, very soon joining a deer fence. If you miss the turning, you will shortly reach a crossing path by an orienteering waypost. In which case, simply turn right to meet the fence. Continue steeply upwards beside it, eventually meeting a junction of paths at the corner of the fence. Turn right, still by the fence and carry on to intersect a

Canoes on the rapids below Symonds Yat

forest road at the next corner.

Go right and then keep left at a fork. With the gradient now eased, the track curves left to a junction **C**. Turn left, but immediately leave right at a waypost for a path, which soon leads to a fork. Near Harkening Rock lies just to the left – a stunning viewpoint out to the Wye Valley. Its concave cliff acts to magnify sound, hence its name, and local tales tell of verderers coming here to listen for poachers.

Return to the fork and now take the other branch, the path dropping abruptly below the cliff and then swinging left beneath the overhang. At the far end a waymark directs you right, again falling steeply and passing the Suck Stone before reaching a forest road. The massive boulder of conglomerate, reputed to be the largest in Britain has been estimated to weigh as much as 14,000 tons.

Head left, walking for almost ½ mile before finding a discretely waymarked path that forks off left at the corner of a deer fence. Climb beside it to reach a higher path and follow that right, continuing beyond the end of the fence. Eventually approaching the edge of the forest, dip right and then keep left to climb back behind houses where you will find an ancient well dedicated to John the Baptist. Until mains water arrived in 1931, the spring served as one of the main sources of water for the village.

Walk out to the main road at the edge of Staunton **D**, crossing to a lane diagonally opposite. Immediately after passing through a gate, take a path off on the right, which settles in a gentle climb beside a low stone wall at the edge of Rodge Wood. Stick with it all the way to the top, there passing through it to reach the Buck Stone **E**. Yet another of the forest's spectacular cliff-top viewpoints, it gazes across the valley to a distant horizon of the Black Mountains. The boulder at your feet once rocked, giving it its name. But a party of Victorian revellers gave it an over-enthusiastic push, dislodging it from its plinth from which it fell in pieces. It has since been put back together and is now firmly secured in place.

Return through the wall and bear right, following a downhill track that curves below the covered hilltop reservoir. Joining a lane at the bottom, go left, but where that then bends sharply right, keep ahead through a corner of woodland, simply cutting off a corner before rejoining the lane. At the end go right, staying with the main lane as it then bends left. At the next junction bear right, walking up towards the main road opposite Staunton's church.

Approaching the stepped cross **❻**, turn off right along a restricted byway beside Church Cottage, later bearing right at a junction. Reaching a bend a little farther on, ignore the grass track off right and keep ahead, climbing into

Looking out from Near Harkening Rock

woodland. After a while, meeting a broad forest track, go left, walking down to a second junction where you should go left again. Then, reaching a T-junction, take a narrow waymarked path opposite, which soon leads to the main road.

Cross diagonally right to a tall standing stone, also known as the Long Stone **❼**. Dating from the Bronze Age, it stands over 7 feet high and tradition says that it will bleed if pricked exactly on the stroke of midnight.

Follow the path beside it into the forest, ignoring a crossing path to meet a forest road. Turn right and at a junction follow the path ahead. At the next junction go left, and, ignoring side paths keep with it until, in time you meet another broad forest track. Walk right through a barrier and straight away turn off left, passing a cottage to reach another junction of paths opposite a campsite. Go left, following the perimeter until you eventually emerge onto a lane **❽**.

Cross diagonally right to a track opposite and bear right on a waymarked path. Ignore a diagonally

crossing track at Hillersland, again keeping ahead at a second junction a little farther on to pass around a cottage and smallholding. Disregard the path off right and keep going, another track joining from the left before you arrive at a narrow lane. Follow the ongoing track facing you, which soon leads to a tarmac drive at the entrance to the Symonds Yat car park. Go left back to the start.

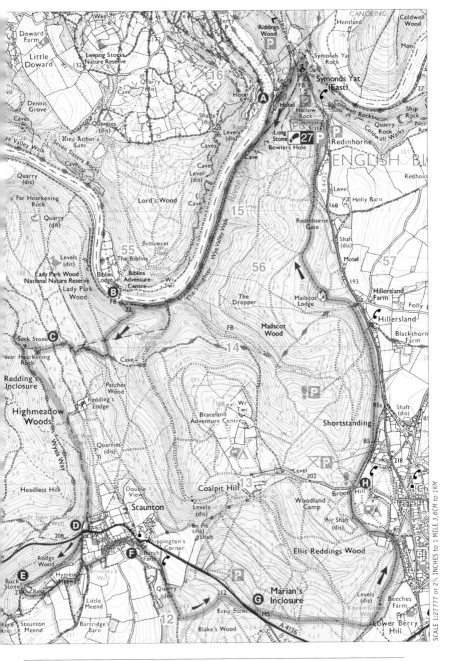

The Upper Honddu Horseshoe

		GPS waypoints
Start	Gospel Pass	✎ SO 236 350
Distance	10½ miles (16.9km)	**A** SO 244 366
Height gain	1,920 feet (585m)	**B** SO 270 319
Approximate time	5½ hours	**C** SO 263 310
Parking	Parking area at start	**D** SO 257 311
Route terrain	Hill paths, including a very steep	**E** SO 253 317
	descent	**F** SO 249 319
Ordnance Survey maps	Landranger 161 (The Black	**G** SO 224 350
	Mountains), Explorer OL13 (Brecon Beacons National	
	Park – Eastern area)	

Twmpa, otherwise known as Lord Hereford's Knob, is a prominent outcrop along the rearing escarpment defining the north western edge of the Black Mountains and, with neighbouring Hay Bluff, overlooks the Wye Valley above Hay-on-Wye. Beginning on the saddle between the two, this walk links the hills in a superb ridge walk, which drops steeply into the valley at Capel-y-ffin.

Gospel Pass stands at the head of a long and beautiful valley, the Vale of Ewyas, a classic example of the power of glaciation. Its name dates from the 12th century when Baldwin, Archbishop of Canterbury passed through in his mission to further the cause of the Third Crusade. He was accompanied by the observant and, occasionally, witty chronicler Gerald of Wales, who described the valley as 'shut in on all sides by a lofty circle of mountains and which is no more than three arrow-shots in width'.

✎ From the parking area, briefly follow the lane towards the top of Gospel Pass before bearing right on a path that curves into a stiff pull up the rim above Blaendigedi. The gradient soon lessens to continue more easily uphill, eventually joining Offa's Dyke

Path, which has tackled the escarpment head-on from the bottom car park. Keep going to the triangulation pillar marking the summit of Hay Bluff **A**.

The panorama on a clear day is simply stunning and west of north looks out across the Wye Valley to the far-off Cambrian Mountains. Plynlimon, lies over 40 miles to the north west, from whose slopes springs the source of the River Wye. Panning clockwise brings in the distant Shropshire hills with the gentle undulations of the Herefordshire countryside closer to. Twmpa lies to the south west, over which the walk will return at the end of the day.

The onward route follows the Offa's Dyke Path south east along the broad ridge. The path is wide and well made, so there is little danger of becoming lost, but even so, these bleak uplands deserve respect, particularly in winter conditions. For a time the way runs undemandingly across the moor, but after a

Black Mountain ponies

junction, from which a path drops into the Olchon Valley, the ridge slowly rises to the highest point of the walk. Beyond, enjoy a long, gentle descent, before another short pull over a crest above Capel-y-ffin. After another ¼ mile, you come to a stone waypost indicating a path off right to Capel-y-ffin **B**.

Take your last look into the Olchon Valley and head down the hill. The path is clear, but falls ever more steeply above the head of Nant Vision. Lower down, watch for it swinging sharply left into zigzags that attempt to lessen the abrupt slope. *Take particular care in wet weather, for the grass path can be slippery.*

Eventually, a final turn of the path levels it alongside the intake wall, following it down to a stile. A path drops straight through a pleasant wood to emerge onto a lane at the bottom **C**. Turn right through a gate, rising past farm buildings and continuing beyond along a lovely sunken lane. Crossing a stream, Nant-y-Ffin swing down left past the abandoned steading of Ty-Shores to the Afon Honddu. On the far bank, rise to meet the valley lane **D**. Follow it right into the tiny hamlet of Capel-y-ffin, keeping right to pass the old church.

Translated from the beautifully descriptive place-name language of the Welsh, Capel-y-ffin means chapel on

the boundary, the boundary perhaps being that separating the bishoprics of St David's and Llandaf. The church, white painted and topped with a lopsided wooden bell cote, is dedicated to St Mary and was built in 1762 to replace a medieval chapel. It has a lovely setting amid a graveyard of ancient yews and leaning tombstones. The Victorian diarist and clergyman, Francis Kilvert, who served at both Clyro and Bredwardine, described it as 'the old chapel, short, stout and boxy, with its little bell turret, squatting like a stout grey owl among its seven great yews'; wonderfully apt. Although one of the smallest chapels in the country, it manages to squeeze in a balcony and no stained-glass creation could rival the simple views through its tiny plain-glass windows.

Among the churchyard memorials are two by Eric Gill, who came to live in the village in 1924. Hailed as the first of the modern British sculptors, his creations ranged from the sublimely religious to outrageously erotic. Gill's artistic work was influential and extended to design and calligraphy, and among other things, he decorated the definitive stamps issued for George VI and designed several typefaces including Gill Sans.

Carry on up the lane for another 200

yds before leaving left over a waymarked stile beside a gate **E**. Climb away up the middle of a meadow towards cottages at Pen-y-maes. Walk between the cottages, passing through a gate and over a stile to continue through a fringe of woodland above. At a junction just above the trees **F**, go right, steadily gaining height along the side of the hill.

Take the higher path at a fork a little farther on, the way raking more steeply upwards before doubling back towards the snout of the ridge. Swinging right, keep climbing, soon reaching a short stone wall shelter. It is a great spot to dally and enjoy the view down the valley, where there is the ruin of an abbey.

William de Lacy, who founded the first priory at Llanthony was not the only one inspired by the valley's spiritual serenity and in 1870, the foundation stone for a new monastery was laid above Capel-y-ffin. Called Llanthony Tertia to distinguish it from the priory down the valley and its daughter house in Gloucester, the abbey was the effectuation of the self-styled Father Ignatius Lyne to revive Benedictine monasticism within the Anglican Church. He inspired a small band of monks, nuns and lay followers who, because of a shortage of funds, undertook much of the work themselves. Their craftsmanship, however, fell far short of their faith and the building has failed the test of time, as did the community, which disbanded after Lyne's death in 1908. Although unorthodox, Lyne was something of a charismatic figure and the ruined church became a place of annual pilgrimage following visions of the

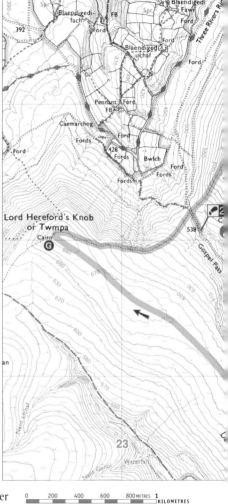

Virgin Mary to Lyle and his monks labouring in the fields.

With the bulk of the climb accomplished, you can adopt a relaxed plod along the ridge. A magnificent all-round view opens, the narrower ridge lending a greater intimacy to the scene than that experienced earlier in the day. Eventually Twmpa's cairn appears ahead, finely crafted from small, flat stones.

From the cairn **G**, the way off lies along the clear path leaving sharp right, an enjoyable loping descent, which leads back to the lane at Gospel Pass. ●

Further Information

 ## Walking Safety

Although the reasonably gentle countryside that is the subject of this book offers no real dangers to walkers at any time of the year, it is still advisable to take sensible precautions and follow certain well-tried guidelines.

Always take with you both warm and waterproof clothing and sufficient food and drink. Wear suitable footwear, such as strong walking boots or shoes that give a good grip over stony ground, on slippery slopes and in muddy conditions. Try to obtain a local weather forecast and bear it in mind before you start. Do not be afraid to abandon your proposed route and return to your starting point in the event of a sudden and unexpected deterioration in the weather.

All the walks described in this book will be safe to do, given due care and respect, even during the winter. Indeed, a crisp, fine winter day often provides perfect walking conditions, with firm ground underfoot and a clarity unique to this time of the year. The most difficult hazard likely to be encountered is mud, especially when walking along woodland and field paths, farm tracks and bridleways – the latter in particular can often get churned up by cyclists and horses. In summer, an additional difficulty may be narrow and overgrown paths, particularly along the edges of cultivated fields. Always ensure appropriate footwear is worn.

 ## Walkers and the Law

The Countryside and Rights of Way Act (CRoW Act 2000) extends the rights of access previously enjoyed by walkers in England and Wales. Implementation of these rights began on 19 September 2004. The Act amends existing legislation and for the first time provides access on foot to certain types of land – defined as mountain, moor, heath, down and registered common land.

Where You Can Go
Rights of Way
Prior to the introduction of the CRoW Act, walkers could only legally access the countryside along public rights of way. These are either 'footpaths' (for walkers only) or 'bridleways' (for walkers, riders on horseback and pedal cyclists). A third category called 'Byways open to all traffic' (BOATs), is used by motorised vehicles as well as those using non-mechanised transport. Mainly they are green lanes, farm and estate roads, although occasionally they will be found crossing mountainous area.

Rights of way are marked on Ordnance Survey maps. Look for the green broken lines on the Explorer maps, or the red dashed lines on Landranger maps.

The term 'right of way' means exactly what it says. It gives a right of passage over what, for the most part, is private land. Under pre-CRoW legislation walkers were required to keep to the line of the right of way and not stray onto land on either side. If you did inadvertently wander off the right of way, either because of faulty map reading or because the route was not clearly indicated on the ground, you were technically trespassing.

Local authorities have a legal obligation to ensure that rights of way are kept clear and free of obstruction, and are signposted where they leave metalled roads. The duty of local authorities to install signposts extends to the placing of signs along a path or way, but only where the authority considers it necessary to have a signpost or waymark to assist persons unfamiliar with the locality.

The New Access Rights
Access Land
As well as being able to walk on existing rights of way, under the new legislation you now have access to large areas of open land. You can of course continue to use rights of way footpaths to cross this land, but the main difference is that you can now

Countryside Access Charter

Further Information

Your rights of way are:

- public footpaths – on foot only. Sometimes waymarked in yellow
- bridle-ways – on foot, horseback and pedal cycle. Sometimes waymarked in blue
- byways (usually old roads), most 'roads used as public paths' and, of course, public roads – all traffic has the right of way

Use maps, signs and waymarks to check rights of way. Ordnance Survey Explorer and Landranger maps show most public rights of way

On rights of way you can:

- take a pram, pushchair or wheelchair if practicable
- take a dog (on a lead or under close control)
- take a short route round an illegal obstruction or remove it sufficiently to get past

You have a right to go for recreation to:

- public parks and open spaces – on foot
- most commons near older towns and cities – on foot and sometimes on horseback
- private land where the owner has a formal agreement with the local authority

In addition you can use the following by local or established custom or consent, but ask for advice if you are unsure:

- many areas of open country, such as moorland, fell and coastal areas, especially those in the care of the National Trust, and some commons
- some woods and forests, especially those owned by the Forestry Commission
- country parks and picnic sites
- most beaches
- canal towpaths
- some private paths and tracks Consent sometimes extends to horse-riding and cycling

For your information:

- county councils and London boroughs maintain and record rights of way, and register commons
- obstructions, dangerous animals, harassment and misleading signs on rights of way are illegal and you should report them to the county council
- paths across fields can be ploughed, but must normally be reinstated within two weeks
- landowners can require you to leave land to which you have no right of access
- motor vehicles are normally permitted only on roads, byways and some 'roads used as public paths'

lawfully leave the path and wander at will, but only in areas designated as access land.

Where to Walk

Areas now covered by the new access rights – Access Land – are shown on Ordnance Survey Explorer maps bearing the access land symbol on the front cover.

'Access Land' is shown on Ordnance Survey maps by a light yellow tint surrounded by a pale orange border. New orange coloured 'i' symbols on the maps will show the location of permanent access information boards installed by the access authorities.

Restrictions

The right to walk on access land may lawfully be restricted by landowners. Landowners can, for any reason, restrict access for up to 28 days in any year. They cannot however close the land:

- on bank holidays;
- for more than four Saturdays and Sundays in a year;
- on any Saturday from 1 June to 11 August; or
- on any Sunday from 1 June to the end of September.

They have to provide local authorities with five working days' notice before the date of closure unless the land involved is an area of less than five hectares or the closure is for less than four hours. In these cases landowners only need to provide two hours' notice.

Whatever restrictions are put into place on access land they have no effect on existing rights of way, and you can continue to walk on them.

Dogs

Dogs can be taken on access land, but must be kept on leads of two metres or less between 1 March and 31 July, and at all times where they are near livestock. In addition landowners may impose a ban on all dogs from fields where lambing takes place for up to six weeks in any year. Dogs may be banned from moorland used for grouse shooting and breeding for up to five years.

In the main, walkers following the routes in this book will continue to follow existing rights of way, but a knowledge and understanding of the law as it affects walkers, plus the ability to distinguish access land marked on the maps, will enable anyone who wishes to depart from paths that cross access land either to take a shortcut, to enjoy a view or to explore.

General Obstructions

Obstructions can sometimes cause a problem on a walk and the most common of these is where the path across a field has been ploughed over. It is legal for a farmer to plough up a path provided that it is restored within two weeks. This does not always happen and you are faced with the dilemma of following the line of the path, even if this means treading on crops, or walking round the edge of the field. Although the latter course of action seems the most sensible, it does mean that you would be trespassing.

Other obstructions can vary from overhanging vegetation to wire fences across the path, locked gates or even a cattle feeder on the path.

Use common sense. If you can get round the obstruction without causing damage, do so. Otherwise only remove as much of the obstruction as is necessary to secure passage.

If the right of way is blocked and cannot be followed, there is a long-standing view that in such circumstances there is a right to deviate, but this cannot wholly be relied on.

Although it is accepted in law that highways (and that includes rights of way) are for the public service, and if the usual track is impassable, it is for the general good that people should be entitled to pass into another line. However, this should not be taken as indicating a right to deviate whenever a way is impassable. If in doubt, retreat.

Report obstructions to the local authority and/or the Ramblers.

 ## Useful Organisations

**Campaign for the Protection
of Rural Wales**
Tŷ Gwyn, 31 High Street,
Welshpool
SY21 7YD
Tel. 01938 552525/556212
www.cprw.org.uk

Campaign to Protect Rural England
128 Southwark Street,
London SE1 0SW
Tel. 020 7981 2800
www.cpre.org.uk

Camping and Caravanning Club
Greenfields House,
Westwood Way, Coventry
CV4 8JH
Site bookings Tel. 0845 130 7633
www.campingandcaravanningclub.co.uk

Countryside Council for Wales
Maes-y-Flynnon,
Penrhosgarnedd,
Bangor LL57 2DW
Tel. 0845 130 6229
www.ccw.gov.uk

Forestry Commission
Silvan House, 231 Corstorphine Road,
Edinburgh EH12 7AT
Tel. 0131 334 0303
www.forestry.gov.uk
Forest of Dean:
Bank House, Bank Street, Coleford,

Gloucestershire GL16 8BA
Tel. 01594 833057

Long Distance Walkers' Association
www.ldwa.org.uk

National Trust
Membership and general enquiries:
PO Box 39, Warrington
WA5 7WD
Tel. 0844 800 1895
www.nationaltrust.org.uk
Wales Regional Office:
Trinity Square,
Llandudno
LL30 2DE
Tel: 01492 860123
West Midlands Regional Office:
Attingham Park, Shrewsbury
SY4 4TP
Tel. 01743 708100

Natural England
1 East Parade,
Sheffield S1 2ET
Tel. 0300 060 6000
www.naturalengland.org.uk

Ordnance Survey
Tel. 08456 05 05 05
www.ordnancesurvey.co.uk

Ramblers
2nd Floor, Camelford House,
87-90 Albert Embankment,
London SE1 7TW
Tel. 020 7339 8500
www.ramblers.org.uk
Wales Regional Office:
3 Coopers Yard, Curran Road,
Cardiff CF10 5NB
Tel. 0292 064 4308

Tourist information:
Heart of England
www.visitheartofengland.com
Visit Wales

Tel. 08708 300 306
www.visitwales.co.uk

Youth Hostels Association
Trevelyan House,
Dimple Road,
Matlock
DE4 3YH
Tel. 0800 0191 700
www.yha.org.uk

Ordnance Survey maps of the Wye Valley and Forest of Dean

The Wye Valley and Forest of Dean area is covered by Ordnance Survey 1:50 000 ($1\frac{1}{4}$ inches to 1 mile or 2cm to 1km) scale Landranger map sheets 148, 149, 161, 162 and 172. These all-purpose maps are packed with information to help you explore the area. Viewpoints, picnic sites, places of interest, caravan and camping sites are shown, as well as public rights of way information such as footpaths and bridleways.

To examine this area in more detail, and especially if you are planning walks, Ordnance Survey Explorer maps at 1:25 000 ($2\frac{1}{2}$ inches to 1 mile or 4cm to 1km) scale are ideal:

OL13 (Brecon Beacons National Park – Eastern area)
OL14 (Wye Valley & Forest of Dean)
189 (Hereford & Ross-on-Wye)
190 (Malvern Hills & Bredon Hill)

To get to the Wye Valley, use the Ordnance Survey Great Britain OS Travel Map-Route at 1:625 000 (1 inch to 10 miles or 4cm to 25km) scale or Ordnance Survey OS Travel Map-Road 6 (Wales & West Midlands), at 1:250 000 (1 inch to 4 miles or 1cm to 2.5km) scale.

Ordnance Survey maps and guides are available from most booksellers, stationers and newsagents.